7161 497

☞ **W9-BNO-128**

OPPOSING
VIEWPOINTS®
SERIES

| Athletes, Ethics,
| and Morality

Other Books of Related Interest

Opposing Viewpoints Series
Celebrity Culture
Ethics
Performance-Enhancing Drugs

At Issue Series
Civil Disobedience
Populism in the Digital Age
When Is Free Speech Hate Speech?

Current Controversies Series
Drug Legalization
Medical Ethics
Racial Profiling

> "Congress shall make
> no law ... abridging
> the freedom of speech,
> or of the press."

First Amendment to the US Constitution

The basic foundation of our democracy is the First Amendment guarantee of freedom of expression. The Opposing Viewpoints series is dedicated to the concept of this basic freedom and the idea that it is more important to practice it than to enshrine it.

OPPOSING VIEWPOINTS® SERIES

Athletes, Ethics, and Morality

Martin Gitlin, Book Editor

GREENHAVEN
PUBLISHING

Published in 2019 by Greenhaven Publishing, LLC
353 3rd Avenue, Suite 255, New York, NY 10010

Cover image: Oleg Petrov/Shutterstock.com

Library of Congress Cataloging-in-Publication Data

Names: Gitlin, Marty, editor.
Title: Athletes, ethics, and morality / Martin Gitlin, Book Editor.
Description: First Edition. | New York : Greenhaven Publishing, 2019. |
 Series: Opposing viewpoints | Includes bibliographical references and
 index. | Audience: Grade 9 to 12.
Identifiers: LCCN 2018026330| ISBN 9781534504103 (library bound) | ISBN
 9781534504318 (pbk.)
Subjects: LCSH: Sports--Moral and ethical aspects--Juvenile literature. |
 Athletes--Conduct of life--Juvenile literature.
Classification: LCC GV706.3 .A97 2019 | DDC 796.01--dc23
LC record available at https://lccn.loc.gov/2018026330

Manufactured in the United States of America

Website: http://greenhavenpublishing.com

Contents

Chapter 3: What Responsibility Do Athletes Have to Their Leagues?

Chapter 4: What Responsibility Do Team Owners Have to Their Players?

The Importance of Opposing Viewpoints

Perhaps every generation experiences a period in time in which the populace seems especially polarized, starkly divided on the important issues of the day and gravitating toward the far ends of the political spectrum and away from a consensus-facilitating middle ground. The world that today's students are growing up in and that they will soon enter as active and engaged citizens is deeply fragmented in just this way. Issues relating to terrorism, immigration, women's rights, minority rights, race relations, health care, taxation, wealth and poverty, the environment, policing, military intervention, the proper role of government—in some ways, perennial issues that are freshly and uniquely urgent and vital with each new generation—are currently roiling the world.

If we are to foster a knowledgeable, responsible, active, and engaged citizenry among today's youth, we must provide them with the intellectual, interpretive, and critical-thinking tools and experience necessary to make sense of the world around them and of the all-important debates and arguments that inform it. After all, the outcome of these debates will in large measure determine the future course, prospects, and outcomes of the world and its peoples, particularly its youth. If they are to become successful members of society and productive and informed citizens, students need to learn how to evaluate the strengths and weaknesses of someone else's arguments, how to sift fact from opinion and fallacy, and how to test the relative merits and validity of their own opinions against the known facts and the best possible available information. The landmark series Opposing Viewpoints has been providing students with just such critical-thinking skills and exposure to the debates surrounding society's most urgent contemporary issues for many years, and it continues to serve this essential role with undiminished commitment, care, and rigor.

The key to the series's success in achieving its goal of sharpening students' critical-thinking and analytic skills resides in its title—

Opposing Viewpoints. In every intriguing, compelling, and engaging volume of this series, readers are presented with the widest possible spectrum of distinct viewpoints, expert opinions, and informed argumentation and commentary, supplied by some of today's leading academics, thinkers, analysts, politicians, policy makers, economists, activists, change agents, and advocates. Every opinion and argument anthologized here is presented objectively and accorded respect. There is no editorializing in any introductory text or in the arrangement and order of the pieces. No piece is included as a straw man, an easy ideological target for cheap point scoring. As wide and inclusive a range of viewpoints as possible is offered, with no privileging of one particular political ideology or cultural perspective over another. It is left to each individual reader to evaluate the relative merits of each argument—as he or she sees it, and with the use of ever-growing critical-thinking skills—and grapple with his or her own assumptions, beliefs, and perspectives to determine how convincing or successful any given argument is and how the reader's own stance on the issue may be modified or altered in response to it.

This process is facilitated and supported by volume, chapter, and selection introductions that provide readers with the essential context they need to begin engaging with the spotlighted issues, with the debates surrounding them, and with their own perhaps shifting or nascent opinions on them. In addition, guided reading and discussion questions encourage readers to determine the authors' point of view and purpose, interrogate and analyze the various arguments and their rhetoric and structure, evaluate the arguments' strengths and weaknesses, test their claims against available facts and evidence, judge the validity of the reasoning, and bring into clearer, sharper focus the reader's own beliefs and conclusions and how they may differ from or align with those in the collection or those of their classmates.

Research has shown that reading comprehension skills improve dramatically when students are provided with compelling, intriguing, and relevant "discussable" texts. The subject matter of these collections could not be more compelling, intriguing, or urgently relevant to today's students and the world they are poised to inherit. The anthologized articles and the reading and discussion questions that are included with them also provide the basis for stimulating, lively, and passionate classroom debates. Students who are compelled to anticipate objections to their own argument and identify the flaws in those of an opponent read more carefully, think more critically, and steep themselves in relevant context, facts, and information more thoroughly. In short, using discussable text of the kind provided by every single volume in the Opposing Viewpoints series encourages close reading, facilitates reading comprehension, fosters research, strengthens critical thinking, and greatly enlivens and energizes classroom discussion and participation. The entire learning process is deepened, extended, and strengthened.

For all of these reasons, Opposing Viewpoints continues to be exactly the right resource at exactly the right time—when we most need to provide readers with the critical-thinking tools and skills that will serve them well not only in school but also in their careers and their daily lives as decision-making family members, community members, and citizens. This series encourages respectful engagement with and analysis of opposing viewpoints and fosters a resulting increase in the strength and rigor of one's own opinions and stances. Accordingly, it helps make readers "future ready," and that readiness will pay rich dividends for the readers themselves, the citizenry, our society, and the world at large.

Introduction

> *"When you speak of role models,*
> *when we talk to your kids, everybody*
> *is a role model, everyone, just as*
> *you look at Michael Jordan to be the*
> *terrific athlete he is."*
>
> —*Walter Payton, former*
> *Chicago Bears superstar*
> *running back on athletes*
> *as role models*

Sports are a part of our everyday lives, and they bring joy to millions of people around the world. Cheering for your favorite player or team can be serious business for the most devout of fans, who take sports extremely seriously. Professional sports generates a great amount of revenue, in large part due to media and merchandising rights. In 2014, the North American sports market was $60.5 billion, and it was expected to continue growing substantially each year. This is an industry with tremendous influence over kids and adults alike.

This is also an industry driven by fans. The athletes, general managers, coaches, trainers, and others are doing a job. But it is the fans that give their emotions to the players and teams they love. And it is the fans that hurt the most when sports figures callously look out for number one. Whether they like it or not, athletes bear a great deal of that responsibility. They are the ones that fans raise up as heroes and berate as bums. And part of this responsibility rests on our expectations of ethics and morality.

Debates have raged for generations about the necessity of athletes serving as role models to impressionable youth. It is indeed a chicken-egg conundrum. Many athletes reject the notion, claiming that their talents on the field or court or ice do not warrant such responsibility. Indeed, should parents not direct their children to view philanthropists, teachers, and other stand-up people as role models, rather than athletes? On the other hand, many argue that the role model status of athletes is inescapable. They are role models whether they accept it or not, so they are obligated to live up to that responsibility with behavior of which youth can be proud. Most do. Many don't.

And what about loyalty? One side of the debate insists that athletes care little about the fans of the cities in which they play, jumping at the best financial package in free agency the first chance they get. On the other side is practicality and logic that states that all workers seek greater opportunity, though generally on a less lucrative scale. Should not athletes do what is best for themselves and their families?

After all, did most of them not toil and sweat, honing their skills at the amateur levels to maximize said opportunity? And that leads to another thorny issue with a two-sided debate. Why should college football and basketball players perform for free when they attract millions of fans bringing their universities billions of dollars a year? A growing number of people believe they should be paid. But many also feel that a free education should be reward enough and that some athletes do not appreciate its importance. The millions of less athletically skilled college students that must pay thousands of dollars of debt over the course of a couple of decades certainly do.

A more recent topic of conversation covered here and acted on by the National Football League (NFL) to both the support and chagrin of politically aware fans is the right or wrong of failing to stand for the national anthem before games. The league was placed in a sticky situation. Television viewership has plummeted since the controversy arose, though it has been debated whether the kneeling flap started by San Francisco 49ers quarterback Colin Kaepernick was the primary cause. The NFL decided to mandate that players on the field stand for the anthem. Those who declined would be forced to stay in the locker room. Critics claimed the league had taken a stand based on money rather than morality. After all, is it not an American right to protest? About three-fourths of NFL players are African American. Should they not be able to express their discontent over racism and discrimination, such as what they perceive as unwarranted shootings of black men by police in recent years?

Sports team owners and their quest for the almighty buck at the expense of fans share the spotlight. Many perceive them as holding cities and fan bases hostage, particularly in recent years, by their demands that taxpayers pay for new venues or at least millions of dollars in upgrades of existing facilities. The economic importance of sports franchises to cities—especially to local businesses—forces such measures on ballots, where they are often accepted at figurative gunpoint. It has been reported that professional sports owners boast the financial resources to pay for such undertakings themselves. One could hardly imagine owners of most businesses asking for their offices to be rebuilt through public money, but those who run sports teams understand they have their cities and fans in an untenable situation.

And those who refuse? Just ask the fans of the Baltimore Colts, Cleveland Browns, and Seattle SuperSonics. They remember all too well the pain they felt when their franchises bolted for what their owners perceived as better offers. The attraction of new stadiums or arenas and fan bases hungry for a team have motivated owners to skip town while giving little thought to loyalty and the hearts and minds of those who have supported their teams for generations. The Colts and Browns, for instance, played to weekly Sunday sellouts, yet the teams were taken away from the fans.

Greedy owners and players have even tinkered with competitive balance, particularly in Major League Baseball (MLB), where economic imbalance plays a significant role. The lack of a salary cap in the sport allows the rich to get richer through free agency and the poor to draft well and maximize the effectiveness of their minor league systems or fade from the race by May. Teams such as the New York Yankees, Los Angeles Dodgers, and Boston Red Sox make up for mistakes in drafting by signing the premier free agents to lucrative contracts while their competition simply cannot afford to keep up.

But there is another side to the story. It can be argued that, despite the lack of a salary cap, baseball boasts the greatest balance. While football's New England Patriots and basketball's Golden State Warriors seemingly contend for championships every year, baseball's World Series has most recently featured new teams annually. The MLB playoffs are a crapshoot. Though the economic realities of baseball without a salary cap all but ensure competitive teams in cities such as Boston, New York, and Los Angeles, they don't ensure championships. Meanwhile, small-market clubs such as Kansas City, Tampa Bay, and Cleveland have captured pennants or (in the case of the Royals) World Series titles. So the argument gains steam—should the salaries of athletes be capped?

Debates rage on all these topics. Both sides feel strongly. They boast verbal ammunition for their arguments. In *Opposing Viewpoints: Athletes, Ethics, and Morality,* authors take a wide variety of perspectives in chapters titled "What Responsibilities Do We Place on Athletes?," "Are Athletes Paid Fairly?," "What Responsibility Do Athletes Have to Their Leagues?," and "What Responsibility Do Team Owners Have to Their Players?" Though none offer their views on life-or-death issues, their perspectives illustrate the raging debates surrounding this issue. Sport is not simply a small piece of our culture. It carries along with it both the joy and misery of millions. And that is indeed important.

CHAPTER 1

What Responsibilities Do We Place on Athletes?

Chapter Preface

Many debates, including in the world of sports, are multi-dimensional. The argument raging about athletes as appropriate role models is simply two sided. One side focuses on inevitability: Athletes must behave with impressionable kids in mind because they are role models, whether they like it or not. Millions of young people embrace their sports heroes and are negatively affected when athletes are in the spotlight for bad behavior—at worst, criminal activity. The other side argues that parents should actively direct their children to follow the lives and deeds of those who they believe deserve role model status, such as Mother Teresa or charitable billionaire Warren Buffett.

There is truth to both sides of the debate. Most believe that parents and even teachers must embrace their responsibilities and make a concerted effort to prevent children from perceiving athletes as anything more than gifted entertainers with the same potential flaws as any human. They claim that adults should also inform kids that a large percentage of athletes come from adverse circumstances and that they remain affected by their backgrounds even after gaining wealth by their talents in sports.

Others state the opposite. They cite the fact that parents and teachers cannot be around kids constantly or insist that they not look up to their sports heroes as role models. That argument puts the ball back in the athletes' court. If indeed they are undeniable role models, should they not embrace that critical responsibility? Some athletes make it known that they do not want to be role models. Others publicly acknowledge their desire to be role models and act on it on and off the fields of play.

The debate will never end. It will rage as long as kids follow the exploits of their favorite sports figures.

> *"When dealing with kids, we can't simply slap a label of 'role model' on them and expect them to excel without our guidance and development."*

With Leadership Comes Responsibility

Dr. Chris Stankovich

In the following viewpoint, Dr. Chris Stankovich argues that the role model status that fans assign to sports figures should not be limited to professional athletes. The author believes that student athletes at all levels must be aware of their responsibilities as role models because they have gained respect and admiration through their talents. The author further states that student athletes should appreciate and embrace their status as role models and behave accordingly. This is a difficult lesson, however; student athletes often forget they're being admired by young fans, and they often are young themselves and don't think about their actions. Stankovich is a counselor, professor, media spokesperson, and researcher in the field of sport, exercise, and health psychology.

"Remind Student Athletes That with Leadership Comes Great Responsibility," by Dr. Chris Stankovich, Advanced Human Performance Systems, December 10, 2016. Reprinted by permission.

As you read, consider the following questions:

1. Why does the author think that student athletes should accept the same role model responsibilities as their professional counterparts?
2. What is the strongest argument the author uses here to make his point?
3. What does the author believe are ways that parents and teachers can help student athletes become positive role models?

Student athletes are expected to be role models, and lead their peers through their actions and words. In best-case scenarios kids embrace these expectations, and regularly make healthy decisions and encourage others to do the same. In other instances, however, student athletes have gotten caught up in controversies (or even the law), and failed to live up to the role modeling expectations society has placed on their shoulders. While being a leader is a worthwhile pursuit, not every youngster knows how to lead, nor are they always aware of the magnitude of their decisions as they impact others (for better or for worse). It is for these reasons that we must regularly remind kids that with the title of "leader" comes the big responsibility of owning what that actually means.

The Perks of Being a Leader

Student athletes are afforded many benefits and luxuries as a byproduct of being on a sports team. Being a visible member of the school/community, traveling to different parts of the country, and potentially having part (or all) of their future college paid for in exchange for playing a sport are just a few perks for kids who are committed to sports. Student athletes are often looked at as heroes in their schools and communities, and sometimes opportunities are presented to them that might not have been there had they not been an athlete—especially true for student athletes who embrace being a leader.

"WE ARE CHOSEN"

Back in the spring of 1993, basketball superstar Charles Barkley created a stir when he starred in this Nike television ad.

Barkley made it clear that the role of athletes was simply to perform on the court or field of play. He concluded that he had no moral obligations to be a role model for young people. Barkley is quoted in the controversial spot as saying, "I am not a role model. Parents should be role models. Just because I can dunk a basketball, doesn't mean I should raise your kids."

At the time, many of his fellow athletes disagreed with him. For decades, athletes had been venerated to a higher status in North America and many of them took this obligation seriously. During the subsequent fallout from Barkley's commercial, NBA star Karl Malone was quoted as saying, "Charles … I don't think it's your decision to make. We don't choose to be role models, we are chosen. Our only choice is whether to be a good role model or a bad one."

Recent incidents have many people re-visiting Barkley's commercial from 1993 and applying it to today's athletes. In my opinion, Barkley may have ruffled some feathers 20 years ago, but he was accurate with his statements that athletes aren't role models for children. Kids need to have role models they can interact with on a daily basis and have a meaningful relationship with. This is why parents, teachers, coaches and other adults should be the primary role models in a young person's life. The posters on the walls can't talk back to kids and give them any meaningful tips on how to navigate life. The relationship between an athlete and their fans is skin-deep—limited to sound-bytes on television and carefully crafted PR images.

Athletes may have money, fame and take up a significant amount of your child's screen time—but that doesn't mean you should put any faith in them to be role models outside of the arena or stadium. Teach your kids to enjoy athletes for their work on the field because there is nothing wrong with hero-worshipping from that standpoint.

But if you are looking for moral guidance from a professional athlete, you will be sadly disappointed. When it comes to being an influence on a child's life, parents need to be the stars—not the athletes.

"Why Athletes Should Never Be Role Models for Kids," by Ian Mendes, Rogers Media, September 19, 2014.

The Responsibilities of Being a Leader

The challenge, however, is gaining a full understanding and appreciation of the expectations that accompany being a role model and leader. Student athletes are often held to a higher standard, especially as this applies to their decision-making. Drilling deeper, this includes the parties they choose to attend (especially if alcohol/drugs are present), the academic grades they earn in school, and even the ways in which they use social media. Unfortunately, many student athletes overlook these issues, or minimize their importance.

When dealing with kids, we can't simply slap a label of "role model" on them and expect them to excel without our guidance and development. Some kids simply don't know what being a leader actually means, while other kids like the title of being a leader, but are not fully committed to engaging in leadership behaviors and activities.

How Coaches and Parents Can Help

- Discuss the visibility of being a student athlete. It is important that student athletes realize just how visible they are, as it is quite common for kids to forget/overlook this reality. Student athletes are regularly featured on tv, newspapers, and social media, and when they are in public and wearing their sports gear (i.e. letter winners jacket) it becomes easy for the public to quickly identify them. It is for these reasons that student athletes should always assume they are being watched and monitored since they never know how they are being seen by others.

- Identify specific "leadership" actions and conduct. Another challenge student athletes regularly experience is learning exactly what it means to be a leader. It's interesting in that we quickly ascribe the title of "role model" to kids who play sports, but we don't always teach them exactly what this means, or how to go about being a role model. Is it any wonder why some kids struggle with the expectations of being a leader when they have never been taught exactly what that means? Take time out to teach kids how to use social media constructively, volunteer in the community, and address important concerns at school so that they have tangible examples of leadership in action.

- Examine the many responsibilities that come with role modeling. Along with teaching kids how to be leaders, we should also remind them of the sphere of influence they have over others, and how their decisions impact how others think and behave. This means that the ways in which they conduct themselves should not be taken lightly, and that if they choose to engage in unhealthy and/or illegal behaviors, they will almost certainly inspire others to do the same, unfortunately.

Being a sports role model should be an exciting opportunity for kids, but it's also important that we teach them how to be role models, as well as emphasize how impactful their words and actions are to others watching. When student athletes embrace the role of being a leader and carry out the expectations accordingly, they have a tremendous opportunity to not only affect their teammates, but also their non-athlete peers and entire community at-large.

"It is difficult to see, in a practical sense, how athletes function as community role models if little is known about them outside of sport."

Few People Believe Athletes Are Role Models

Daryl Adair

In the following viewpoint, Daryl Adair argues that the issue of athletes accepting and embracing role model responsibility is prominent in Australia. The author asserts that the status of athletes as role models is overrated, especially regarding sports figures who are not well known outside the sports world. He states his belief that only a small percentage of the public perceives athletes as role models anyway and offers that it is not a significant issue. Adair is an associate professor of sports management at the University of Technology in Sydney.

As you read, consider the following questions:

1. What facts does the author provide that only relatively few people embrace athletes as role models?
2. Do you think that his arguments would prove equally legitimate in the sports-crazy United States?
3. What Muslim soccer player does the author cite in stating his case, and why is his name evoked?

I t has become a truism that professional athletes, whether they like it or not, "are" role models for others. Talented sportspeople hardly win every time, and sometimes they do not exemplify fair play. But many athletes convey attributes about performance, character and resilience that draw admiration from fans.

For the youthful, sports stars may prompt efforts to emulate tries, wickets, goals and baskets in backyards or parks. No surprise, then, that professional athletes are assumed to provide a "role model effect" for sport at community levels, whether by stimulating entry into organised activities or by catalysing ongoing participation.

However, researchers have been ambivalent or unconvinced about the efficacy of a "role model effect" in terms of sport engagement.

For example, the 2012 London Olympics—in which British athletes performed exceptionally well—were staged against the policy backdrop of a "participation legacy"—a concerted strategy to increase physical activity across the UK. Despite the headline performances of medal-winning British athletes, overall sport participation rates fell after the Games.

There is, in short, no logical connection between sport fandom and sport exercise. What's more, the easy assumption that high-performance athletes "inspire" a generation of community-based sport participants is not only unfounded, it is bad policy. That point even applies to sportspeople who have reached the zenith of their profession. In one global survey:

> ... only 10% of the elite athletes have been inspired by other elite athletes in order to start with their current sport. Mostly they were encouraged by their parents (59%) and friends (28%) to practice their current sport.

Athletes as Off-Field Role Models

High-profile athletes are widely feted as public figures outside of sport, as happens with celebrities in other entertainment professions. In sport, though, such recognition is said to come with additional responsibilities, most notably in the assumption that athletes are (or must become) "role models in the community."

In a contractual sense, athletes are employees when representing their club during community events such as school visits, charity fundraisers, and the like. These are occasions when athletes are expected to promote their sport or to support an organisation aligned with their club.

Whether heartfelt or perfunctory, such actions may be construed as inauthentic, much "like the politician kissing a baby."

Beyond these official responsibilities, athletes would be naïve to expect the same level of privacy as someone without a public profile. So there is a trade-off, as happens with notable performers in other spheres of life, such as entertainers or politicians.

However, the off-field obligations of an athlete involve significant surveillance. They must notify a National Anti-Doping Authority where they are every day of the year, and must be available for drug testing from 6am to 11pm. A typical part of athlete contracts is the catch-all phrase of "bringing the game into disrepute," which in practice means that an employer can dismiss an employee for off-field conduct that it deems contrary to the interests of a club or a sport.

In these ways, the off-field expectations of athletes are couched in punitive terms.

Taking a more positive view, it is a common refrain that athletes are role models for, or even in, a wider community. However, this taken-for-granted assumption has not been accompanied by research to explore the efficacy of such claims. There appears to be profound differences between athletes' self-perception as off-field influencers.

NBA star Charles Barkley once declared that he was "not paid to be a role model," and that "parents should be role models." Barkley did not consider himself particularly virtuous as a person, but said that he was well equipped to "wreak havoc on a basketball court."

Role Models with Serious Flaws

Young adults and children idolize athletes. They're considered role models because of their media presence and ability to help or change the lives of those less fortunate. For awhile now, there's been a debate on whether they should be looked at as such.

Each of us has our own talent whether it is playing basketball, baseball or another sport, and we present our craft differently to one another. These athletes are not perfect, so they shouldn't be put on a pedestal because we all have flaws. It makes it worse because their actions are highlighted in the media and people see that and want to imitate it, good or bad.

According to an ABC News article, "three-fourths of the 1,500 10 to 17-year-olds and 1,950 parents surveyed said athletes teach children that being a good sport and playing fair are as important as winning." But the article also stated that children think it's alright to receive special treatment on and off the court, and being promiscuous is alright.

This is teaching children not be held accountable for their actions when in reality they are held accountable. People have forgotten what it means to be a true athlete, being a team player, the reward of hard work, the importance of dedication and enjoying what you love to do, not just for fame and fortune.

Lamar Odom, a retired player for the Los Angeles Lakers and championship winner, struggled with a drug addiction. He was found unconscious and was on life support, but he came out of the coma days later. Odom might not be doing drugs now but that will be attached to his name forever.

Then there is Lance Armstrong, a cyclist and cancer survivor. He was a seven-time winner of the Tour De France before being stripped of those titles because he used performance enhancement drugs.

In the Sportster it said "he not only ruined his name but other team member's careers as well. I'm sure both these players had a following of children and adults that idolized them and wanted to be just like them."

I'm not saying all athletes are not good role models but should be aware of the examples they are setting.

"Should Athletes Be Role Models?" by Michelle Bright, *The Independent***, February 21, 2017.**

By comparison, some athletes have sought an off-field leadership role, particularly when their status as an athlete provides support to like-minded others.

Bachar Houli, an AFL footballer of Muslim faith, has actively sought to engage with the wider Islamic community, and to provide inspiration for Muslim kids who might want to engage in sport. This community engagement role has been supported by Houli's club, and complements his existing position as a multicultural ambassador for the AFL.

Dual Role Models?

More than 30 years after Barkley's declaration that he was unfit to be a role model, there is heightened expectation that all professional athletes, whether they like it or not, are role models both on and off the field. But is this a logical expectation?

As Feezell has argued, "we know about celebrated athletes' exemplary conduct in sport," but "there is nothing intrinsic to athletic participation that merits the status of being a moral exemplar" beyond that sport-specific role.

Clubs and leagues certainly have expectations that athletes will conduct themselves "appropriately" during their private lives. This is underpinned by sports' support for community-focused initiatives such as the White Ribbon Campaign (countering male violence against women) and the Plan B anti-drink-driving promotion.

But it is unclear why athletes have the skills or values to be positioned as custodians of virtue in such initiatives. The underlying assumption appears to be that sport imbues good character. As a consequence, athletes are thought to be "equipped" to exemplify positive character traits both in sport and during their private lives.

Athletes are very visible on the sport field, but much less noticeable outside it. If athletes actually function as role models beyond sport, the public needs some basis upon which to make assessments of their character. Herein lies a problem. As Feezell points out:

… most of us know very little about the athletes whose exploits we admire.

And, therefore, we are not in a position to know if or how they influence others in wider society. This leads to a further problem. The media typically "thrives on scandal and sensationalism," so stories about public figures "gone bad" are much more likely to appear in the press.

Player welfare managers at professional sports clubs find it very difficult to persuade the media to give prominence to "good deeds" by players; news editors are far more interested in detailing off-field misdemeanours.

Ultimately, then, when a small minority of athletes fails to live up to employer and community expectations, the wider sports profession is tarnished as disreputable.

It is difficult to see, in a practical sense, how athletes function as community role models if little is known about them outside of sport, except where—as in the case of Houli—a role as social influencer is both sought and supported.

> *"There was a time when others served as America's role models (civic leaders, clergy, legal and medical experts, etc.). It might be argued that the shift reflects decay in our nation's moral standards."*

Choose Wisely When Considering Role Models

Frank L. Smoll

In the following viewpoint, Frank L. Smoll argues that, although some athletes have been positive role models, the fact that many kids look up to them in that regard indicates that America is heading in the wrong direction. The author believes that more appropriate role models are available to inspire kids, including civic leaders and clergy. On the other hand, he admits that like it or not, children look to athletes as heroes, so those role models should be chosen wisely. The author suggests several qualities that make a good role model. Smoll is a psychology professor at the University of Washington. His research focuses on coaching behaviors in youth sports and on the psychological effects of competition on children and adolescents.

As you read, consider the following questions:

1. How does the author define role models?
2. Why does Frank L. Smoll believe clergy and civic leaders are more appropriate role models than athletes?
3. What quality does the author suggest should be balanced with the virtue of striving for excellence?

The term *role model* is defined as "a person whose behavior, example, or success is or can be emulated by others, especially younger people" (*Random House Dictionary*). Accordingly, a brain surgeon or airline pilot can be a role model for similarly motivated boys and girls. Role models may have a considerable impact on a person's values, education, and chosen training objectives. For example, they have been shown to have significant effects on female students' self-confidence in pursuing careers in science, technology, engineering, and mathematical (STEM) fields.

What About Sport Stars as Role Models?

There's a history of speculation and argument about athletes taking on the status of role models. In 1993, Nike ran a ground-breaking TV commercial from early April through the end of the NBA playoffs. The ad featured Charles Barkley proclaiming "I am not a role model." At the time, he was a superstar hoopster for the Phoenix Suns, and his comment generated quite a stir, as he staunchly defended his position.

What Was So Controversial About What "Sir Charles" Said?

He emphasized that athletes' ability to make baskets or catch touchdown passes has nothing to do with being a role model. That is, having sporting ability doesn't automatically qualify a person to be a role model. Rather, Barkley believed that's a job for parents. I agree and would include teachers and coaches who spend a huge amount of time with kids and influence their upbringing and future success.

Like It or Not, Our Society Has a Strong Dependence on Athletes as Role Models for Children and Adolescents

Athletes are role models whether or not they choose to take on the responsibility, and whether they are good or bad role models. But athlete "hero worship" wasn't always as prevalent as it is today. There was a time when others served as America's role models (civic leaders, clergy, legal and medical experts, etc.). It might be argued that the shift reflects decay in our nation's moral standards.

On the other hand, some exceptional athletes have important messages for their fans. For example, former heavyweight boxing champ Lennox Lewis made a significant contribution to youngsters' understanding of appropriate masculine behavior, when he made a public service announcement that "Real men don't hit women." The point is clear: Athletes have an incredible opportunity to use their celebrity power to positively influence the next generation.

What Are the Qualities That Make an Athlete a Good Role Model?

- *Enthusiastic about being a role model.* The athlete welcomes the platform for promoting positive societal change—a willing crusader for good.
- *Altruistic mission.* The athlete uses the position to share messages of inspiration and hope—a selfless drive to benefit others.
- *Makes a commitment to behaving in ways that reflect high moral values.* The athlete acts in ways that support personal integrity.
- *Presents himself or herself in a realistic and responsible manner.* "I'm not a role model because I'm a superstar jock, but because I'm a great person." The athlete also helps fans realize that

he or she isn't perfect. After all, role models are only people with weaknesses and flaws. They're not immaculate idols.

- *Freely devotes time and energy to community activities.* The athlete makes appearances at neighborhood events, serves on local boards, works with charity organizations, etc.

- *Champions a mastery goal orientation.* The athlete focuses on personal effort and accomplishments instead of making comparisons with others. In a sense, mastery oriented people compare themselves with themselves. They can feel success and satisfaction when they have learned something new, seen skill improvement in themselves, or given maximum effort. Legendary UCLA basketball coach John Wooden captured the essence of a mastery orientation in his famous definition of success: "Success is peace of mind which is a direct result of self-satisfaction in knowing you made the effort to do the best of which you are capable." (For more information, see my *Psychology Today* blog titled "How to Be a Winner".)

- *Possesses a keen sense of empathy.* The athlete has the capacity to share or recognize emotions experienced by others. Empathy involves putting yourself in other people's shoes and seeing how much you can truly understand them. It includes caring for others and having a desire to help them. Empathy motivates pro-social behavior designed to aid in solving communal challenges. As emphasized by Stephen R. Covey, author of *The Seven Habits of Highly Effective People*, "When you show empathy toward others, their defensive energy goes down, and positive energy replaces it. That's when you can get more creative in solving problems."

- *Displays a healthy balance between striving for excellence and having fun in the process.* The athlete promotes the virtues of working hard to achieve goals and the importance of enjoying the journey.

A Word of Caution Is Warranted

Youngsters who believe their sport heroes are the most fantastic people in the world and can do no wrong are vulnerable to disappointment. Why? Because examples of fallen stars are many, such as Alex Rodriguez and Lance Armstrong who admitted to the use of performance enhancing drugs. When a revered athlete goes astray, it can create disillusionment and even trauma. So, here's the bottom line: *Kids shouldn't be allowed to become too attached to athletes as role models.*

> "Apart from cases where athletes
> have broken the law such as
> Oscar Pistorius or OJ Simpson, or
> have blatantly cheated like Lance
> Armstrong or Maria Sharapova,
> should our moral perceptions of
> athletes not be confined to what they
> do on the field?"

Don't Heap the Burden of
Role Model on Athletes

Daniel Gallan

*In the following viewpoint, Daniel Gallan argues that athletes have
enough to concern themselves with—both on and off the fields of play
and trying to maximize their athletic potential—without having to
worry about how their behavior will affect those who idolize them.
The author contends that pushing that status of "role model" on
athletes is unfair to them and also threatens to disappoint those who
use them in that capacity. In short, no one wins when athletes are
set up to be our heroes. Gallan is a freelance sports journalist who
explores the subject from a political, sociological, and cultural lens.*

"Unfair Expectations: Exploring the 'Role Model' Tag Ascribed to Athlete," by Daniel
Gallan, Conqa Group, October 22, 2016. Reprinted by permission.

As you read, consider the following questions:

1. Why does the author compare athletes to politicians?
2. How do our expectations change, depending on the society an athlete represents, according to the viewpoint?
3. Which boxer does the author use to illustrate the dichotomy of professionalism vs. character in the sports world?

While the New Zealand All Blacks celebrated their record breaking 18th consecutive Test victory by beating Australia 37–10 at Eden Park in Auckland this weekend, one man was conspicuous by his absence. You wouldn't have known it, such was the one sided score line in the end, but one of the best players in the world played no part in this historic achievement.

Aaron Smith, undoubtedly the best scrumhalf on the planet, voluntarily made himself unavailable following a disciplinary hearing in which he was asked to explain his actions involving a sex scandal that, in the words of New Zealand Rugby's General Manager, Neil Sorensen, amounted to "serious misconduct."

Last month, while waiting with his teammates to board a plane to South Africa, Smith engaged in a brief tryst with a woman at Christchurch Airport. A married couple noticed the two enter a disabled toilet cubicle where they heard "rhythmic tapping noises." The husband then pulled out his phone and filmed Smith and the woman leave the cubicle before Smith, in official All Black clothing, joined his teammates as if nothing had happened.

Despite initial plans to keep the information to themselves, the couple reported the incident. "I've never reported anything to a newspaper or anything," the wife said. "We don't want to convey the fact that we're narking or gossiping about his private life. However, the All Blacks are put on a pedestal and are role models for young Kiwis."

She then went on to add, "As such, they should be held to a higher level of scrutiny. Most people would not do that, let alone a public figure."

These sentiments raise a number of concerns. Firstly, to suggest that Smith's actions are beyond "most people" is absurd. Public sex and adultery are obviously regularly occurring phenomenon and millions of people around the world who are not "public figures" cheat on their partners and/or do so in public spaces. That is not to say that cheating is justifiable, simply that it is unfortunately not rare.

Secondly, the notion that the married couple felt they had a right to "nark" on Smith by virtue of the fact that he is an All Black—arguably the highest position of honour a New Zealand man can achieve—leads us down a moral and ethical quandary. If this was any other pair that the married couple happened upon, it is hard to imagine that they would have made the footage public. In some way they felt they had a moral obligation to society to expose Smith and make an example of him for the collective good.

But was this fair? Elite athletes are no doubt placed on pedestals, and it doesn't get any more elite than an All Black, but surely they are placed there first and foremost as a result of their athletic prowess. Apart from cases where athletes have broken the law such as Oscar Pistorius or OJ Simpson, or have blatantly cheated like Lance Armstrong or Maria Sharapova, should our moral perceptions of athletes not be confined to what they do on the field?

For Mike McInerney, a sports psychologist and co-director of Headstrong, a sports psychology and performance organisation operating out of Cape Town, we ascribe the tag of "role model" to our athletes and feel invested in their actions as a result of a sense of ownership. He believes that this ties in with the post-modern amalgamation of the roles of athlete and celebrity and argues that by virtue of them operating in the public's eye, we feel empowered to claim ownership over their image and, by extension, their actions.

"Athletes are demanded not just to produce on the field, but perform a certain role off it," McInerney says. "Our athletes represent the ideals that are valued in society and all too often we are idealistic in terms of what we expect from them."

Smith is 27 years old, at his peak physically and enjoys a level of fame few of us will ever come close to experiencing. Is it that inconceivable that he made this poor error in judgement? Let he who knows what it's like to be a superstar All Black cast the first stone.

But athletes are not the only figures who perform in full view of the public and yet society holds them to a standard not reserved for any other industry. Politicians are in the public eye and yet their after-hour endeavours seem to have less impact on their job security than that of sports stars. Oftentimes, even if politicians are found to have operated poorly at their job they still manage to hold on to their position.

South Africa's President, Jacob Zuma, won over 60% of the vote in the 2014 national elections despite a laundry list of corruption allegations. Donald Trump, the United States presidential hopeful, somehow still has a chance of winning the keys to the Oval Office despite a slew of reprehensible comments aimed at women and minorities.

Film stars, musicians, socialites; in the world of Dan Bilzerian and Kim Kardashian, where people can become famous for twerking on Twitter, it seems lofty ethical standards and expectations are reserved for athletes. Why?

According to Dr Gill Lines in a paper titled, Villains, fools or heroes? Sports stars as role models for young people (2001), she states that the "sporting hero has traditionally been perceived as epitomizing social ideas … and as embodying values which learnt on the playing fields will readily transfer into everyday life."

This is the enduring myth of the "Amateur Gentleman" and "Muscular Christian" of the Victorian era that was brought up in the English public school system and educated in the arts of conduct and chivalry on the sports field. Values such as honour, hard work, respect for the game and fair play are still valued today, but the characteristics of the performing athletes have shifted dramatically with a rapidly changing world.

We don't live our lives according to 19th century standards—certainly the post-modern celebrity does not. However, as Lines states, "such lingering values of sporting heroes continue suggesting sports stars should maintain traditional social standards both on and off the pitch."

That is why the married couple felt emboldened to expose Smith. It was not that they necessarily believed that what Smith did was wrong, but within the context of him being an All Black, and especially while wearing the Silver Fern on his chest, they felt they had a duty as red blooded Kiwis to out this villain.

As Lines says, "If elite sportsman can no longer embody this [our ideal values], then legitimation of such values come under threat." Looking at ourselves in the mirror is a lot harder than trying to see athletes as the flawed humans they are. We hold to the notion that if they display their humanity in a way that upsets us, it is them who must toe the line rather than we who must change our viewpoint.

It's crucial to note that the values that we expect our athletes to uphold will vary depending on the society they represent. Tim Tebow, currently an outfielder with the New York Mets and previously an NFL quarterback, embodies the wholesome Christian image that the southern states of the US cherish. The son of Baptist missionaries, Tebow became famous for praying on one knee before, during and after football matches. He has even been caught on film allegedly reviving a man suffering from a seizure with nothing but the power of prayer.

Compare this image to the hyper-masculine, beer guzzling Australian cricketer of the 1980s. These true blue Aussie blokes, with open collars and facial hair, epitomised the bombastic culture of their country. Even when elite sport realised that downing several cold ones a night might negatively impact performance, the same braggadocio mindset persisted.

However, as we have seen with San Francisco 49ers quarterback, Colin Kaepernick taking a stand against police brutality on African American citizens, polarised opinions can still exist within the same society.

"Athletes are beholden to sponsors to represent their brand but we are also stakeholders and we want our athletes to represent us," McInerney says. "The character traits of the athletes, the methods used to take a stand and the issues they take a stand against will differ from society to society, and from person to person, but the demand to meet those expectations will be just as strong no matter the context."

This also applies from sport to sport. If an Australian Rules footballer acts like a hot head and swears at an opponent, his actions are easily dismissed as a part of the game. However, when Australian tennis star, Nick Kyrgios insults Stan Wawrinka's girlfriend on the court, that is universally unacceptable.

Certain sports like tennis and golf, and to a lessening extent, cricket, still carry an air of the old world. That is why the brother of Danny Willet, the English golfer who represented Europe in the recent Ryder Cup, described US golf fans as the "angry, unwashed Make America Great Again swarm" in reference to their lude and overtly antagonistic behaviour.

The Willets grew up in Sheffield, a South Yorkshire city famous for its steel production and football teams. If the Willets ever attended a Wednesday-United derby, there is no doubt that he would have heard vulgar language from sports fans. In football it's acceptable. In other sports it's just not cricket.

These extra pressures to perform a role both on and off the field can have obvious negative implications. Anything that shifts focus away from performance has the potential to negatively impact how you perform but if used correctly, the role model tag can be used to improve performance.

We've already spoken about how Grant Lottering uses the knowledge that he was raising money for charity to help him achieve the monumental feat of cycling close to 1000km over 48 hours in the Alps. The same has been said about Team Dimension Data riders in the Tour de France.

The Connect Sports Academy is a sports development programme from the Khayelitsha Township in the Western Cape, South Africa and is committed to transform the sporting landscape in the country. At the coalface of one of South Africa's most important issues, this organisation helps young children from disadvantaged backgrounds and provides them with a holistic set of skills to make it in the sports world. After just two full seasons, several young players have been selected to represent their province.

Murray Ingram is the development strategist at Connect and explains how being a role model helps improve on field play. "A lot of the kids come from backgrounds and communities that are affected by the perils of alcohol, abuse, drugs and gangs," Ingram says. "We tell the youngsters that they are pioneers and that they are playing for more than just their own careers. It's not just athletic responsibilities that they have but also moral and social responsibilities. This drives them to raise their performances on match day and in training sessions."

Ingram goes on, "We have to remember that they are kids and they will make mistakes. But we've found that some of the children that came to us with severe behavioural problems as a result of their background are the ones that are now leaders. They are the ones who understand what's at stake. I think being a role model means knowing that you are in a position of privilege and that your standing can impact the lives of others."

So are athletes then obligated to be role models? Floyd Mayweather is arguably the greatest pound for pound boxer of all time with a record of 49–0 with 26 knockouts. He was a tireless professional who worked extremely hard at his craft and yet his demeanour outside of the ring was borderline distasteful. Throw in the fact that he is a serial domestic abuser and you have the perfect example of a dichotomous figure who was the consummate professional but a deplorable character.

For McInerney, an athlete should only ever seek to be a role model if the tag fits in with his or her values. "Motivation is closely linked to what a person's values are," he says. "People are less likely to be motivated if their values don't align with what they're doing."

Integrity is closely linked with honesty and an athlete that presents one image but then acts in a contradictory manner is more likely to lose our respect than an athlete that is upfront with their reluctance to assume the position of a role model. This is why when Hansie Cronje, the former South African cricket captain, was exposed as a match fixer, it hit the country hard. It went against the wholesome, golden boy image he had projected.

Contrast the case of Charles Barkley, the former NBA star, who proudly stated, "I am not a role model. I am not paid to be a role model. I am paid to wreak havoc on the basketball court. Parents should be role models. Just because I dunk a basketball doesn't mean I should raise your kids."

Barkley said that in a Nike advert, the same Nike that cut Tiger Wood's annual endorsement in half as punishment for having an extra-marital affair. In the commercial realm, much like the wider sporting landscape, integrity and honesty are valued even if the root attributes of the athlete are not necessarily righteous.

There is no escaping the fact that sports stars are held to a higher standard than the average person. However, despite our idealism, the majority of athletes, like the majority of all people, are unworthy of the role model tag. We as the public need to be far more selective with regards to who we look up to. In this way, we will be able to see our athletes as the flawed humans they are, and they in turn will be able to focus their attention where it matters—on the field of play.

> *"So you mean to tell me we should now have to watch these overpaid athletes make this a political platform every week instead of just seeing them perform in a sport we love to watch?"*

Athletes Should Not Protest on the Field

Joe Elerson

In the following viewpoint, Joe Elerson expresses his disgust with NFL players who have kneeled during the national anthem. These players have been taking a knee during the anthem as a respectful form of protest. However, the author does not address the specific reasons behind the protests. He instead describes the act of kneeling during the anthem as a slap in the face to fans and the US military and calls on the league to take action (which it did in May 2018). The author does not acknowledge the question of the basic American right to protest, stating only that freedom of speech should not include taking a knee during the anthem. Elerson is a sportswriter for the Athens Daily Review.

"Kneeling During the National Anthem Is Not Acceptable," by Joe Elerson, *Athens Daily Review*, September 29, 2017. Reprinted by permission.

As you read, consider the following questions:

1. Does the author cover all angles in his argument against kneeling for the anthem?
2. Why does the author not perceive kneeling as an American right to protest?
3. According to this viewpoint, does the league have the right to stop players from kneeling, as it did in 2018?

Attention NFL, we have a problem. The protests during the national anthem have gotten out of hand. As a football fan, I was almost ready to change the channel heading into the Sunday night game between Oakland and Washington last week.

It was not because of the fact it was a game I did not care to watch. It was because of all of the coverage of the protests before the games.

I understand people have rights to express their feelings when it comes to freedom of speech. But when it comes to taking a knee during the greatest song we hear prior to games, that is unacceptable.

When you add up the numbers from last Sunday, about one in eight NFL players did not stand for the national anthem. The previous week, only six NFL players protested, continuing the movement started last year by former San Francisco quarterback Colin Kaepernick.

Kaepernick, who is no longer in the NFL, kneeled during the national anthem to protest police violence against African Americans, a fact that two-thirds of Americans knew.

So you mean to tell me we should now have to watch these overpaid athletes make this a political platform every week instead of just seeing them perform in a sport we love to watch?

I don't have an issue with locking arms and standing during the anthem. I am fine with the way the Dallas Cowboys handled their form of protest by kneeling prior to the anthem.

"EVERYONE SHOULD STAND"

"Everyone should stand" during the national anthem, NFL Commissioner Roger Goodell wrote in a memo to all 32 teams, adding that the NFL will present a plan next week to help "move past this controversy."

In the memo sent Tuesday, Goodell said he is "very proud of our players and owners who have done the hard work over the past year to listen, understand and attempt to address the underlying issues within their communities" and expressed respect for players' "opinions and concerns about critical social issues."

And yet, Goodell writes, "like many of our fans, we believe that everyone should stand for the National Anthem ... We want to honor our flag and our country and our fans expect that of us."

"The controversy over the Anthem is a barrier to having honest conversations and making real progress on the underlying issues. We need to move past this controversy, and we want to do that together with our players."

Team owners are scheduled to discuss the plan with Goodell at a meeting next week in New York.

President Trump, who for weeks has been critical of players who kneel, responded to Goodell's memo early Wednesday: "It is

I would hope the players understand that once you take a knee during the national anthem, you are not protesting the government or the leader of the country but the soldiers and veterans who fought for this country to give you the rights you believe you deserve.

A study shows that 57 percent of Americans believe the NFL should not fire athletes who kneel during the national anthem, disagreeing with President Donald Trump. But in the NFL's operations manual, it addresses the national anthem this way:

"During the National Anthem, players on the field and bench area should stand at attention, face the flag, hold helmets in their left hand and refrain from talking. The home team should ensure that the American flag is in good condition. It should be pointed about time that Roger Goodell of the NFL is finally demanding that all players STAND for our great National Anthem-RESPECT OUR COUNTRY," Trump tweeted.

The NFL then responded with a statement saying, "Commentary this morning about the Commissioner's position on the anthem is not accurate." The statement, as reported by NFL Media analyst Ian Rapoport, went on to say "there will be a discussion of these issues at the owners meeting next week" and that the NFL is looking "to move from protest to progress, working to bring people together."

While Goodell's memo Tuesday was short on details, it represents an attempt to lay out a clear and consistent leaguewide policy for players.

An NFL spokesman tells *Sports Illustrated* that the game operations manual already states, "During the National Anthem, players on the field and bench area should stand at attention."

Then-San Francisco 49ers quarterback Colin Kaepernick began the practice of kneeling during the anthem last year, telling NFL Media he was "not going to stand up to show pride in a flag for a country that oppresses black people and people of color."

"NFL's Roger Goodell Says Players 'Should Stand' for National Anthem," by Amy Held, National Public Radio Inc. (NPR), October 11, 2017.

out to players and coaches that we continue to be judged by the public in this area of respect for the flag and our country. Failure to be on the field by the start of the National Anthem may result in discipline, such as fines, suspensions, and/or the forfeiture of draft choice(s) for violations of the above, including first offenses."

So where does it say players should be kneeling, staying in the locker room, raising fists in the air or other forms of protest? Also, does it say in your employee handbook that you have the right to kneel during the national anthem when it is played for an event you attend?

In one study, it shows that nearly six in 10 Americans believe that professional athletes should be required to stand during the national anthem. But Roger Goodell, the NFL commissioner, does not seem to agree with this statement. He said earlier this week that "the way we reacted today, and this weekend, made me proud. I'm proud of our league."

Shame on you, Mr. Goodell, and shame on every player who kneeled, stayed in the locker room, sat on the bench or raised a fist during the national anthem.

The thing that has bothered me the most about the protest is having players kneel, especially when a soldier is in front of them. To show blatant disrespect for the soldiers who have fought to give you the right to play the game is something of which every American should be ashamed.

Once you decide to sit on the bench during the anthem, or you do what Buffalo Bills running back Lesean McCoy did by showing the ultimate form of disrespect, is sickening. During the national anthem, McCoy decided to continue his warm-up stretches while the anthem was being played.

That is a classless act in my opinion, and one I will never tolerate as a football fan. I would hope people will boo him every chance they get for the disrespect he has shown.

I am not sure how I will go about watching the NFL this week. Will I get home from church, and watch the normal set of games I get to watch?

That is to be figured out tomorrow. But one thing is for certain: the NFL needs to figure out another way to address this issue.

> *"After Kaepernick first started the*
> *protest last year, he was criticised for*
> *introducing politics into sports. Many*
> *said that football was somehow*
> *sacrosanct, and that it should*
> *be a place where people can rise*
> *above politics."*

Athletes Can Be Agents of Social Change If We Let Them

Clark Mindock

In the following viewpoint, Clark Mindock reports on the controversy in the United States over NFL players taking a knee in protest during the national anthem. The author explains that Colin Kaepernick's symbolic demonstration protesting racial inequality was intended to be respectful to military veterans, yet his careful display has been received as exactly the opposite. The act of kneeling during the national anthem during sporting events has rankled many who see it as unpatriotic and disrespectful. The author goes on to address the history of athletes and activism. Mindock is a US reporter for the British publication the Independent.

"Taking a Knee: Why Are NFL Players Protesting and When Did They Start to Kneel?" by Clark Mindock, The Independent, May 25, 2018. Reprinted by permission.

As you read, consider the following questions:

1. Can the reader detect even the slightest hint of opining in how the author delivers this article?
2. What can be taken from this piece as the primary sports news?
3. What famous quarterback who had indicated support for President Donald Trump criticized him for his reaction to NFL players kneeling during the national anthem?

A fter a wave of players joined in on American football player Colin Kaepernick's protest movement against police brutality last year—morphing the protest into something of direct resistance to Donald Trump after the president weighed in on the issue—the NFL has now announced that teams will be fined if players take a knee during the national anthem.

The contentious move to take a knee during the national anthem before a game, or stand with arms locked in silent protest, follows in a long tradition of sports stars standing up for what they believe to be right—but some charge that it is unpatriotic and that politics should be kept out of sports.

Here's what you need to know.

When Did This All Start?

Kaepernick's protest first occurred 21 months ago, but was not immediately noticed. At that point, he simply sat on the benches during the US national anthem during a preseason game, just next to the giant Gatorade jugs next to him.

But, he later transitioned to taking a knee in protest—saying he was doing so to show more respect for military veterans—which turned out to be a much more iconic pose. Several other players joined his protest, even though they received a lot of criticism from football fans who said that it was disrespectful to the United States. Still, the movement did not gain huge traction last year.

"I am not going to stand up to show pride in a flag for a country that oppresses black people, and people of color," Kaepernick said in a press conference after first sitting out during the anthem. "To me, this is bigger than football, and it would be selfish on my part to look the other way. There are bodies in the street, and people getting paid leave, and getting away with murder."

What Was the Context Surrounding Those First Protests?

Police brutality has become an incredibly polarising and contentious issue in American life. This has come as a result of repeated videos showing police shooting and killing unarmed black men, which have been posted online and gone viral—illustrating the brutality that black people in America must contend with when dealing with some police officers, who often do not serve any prison time for pulling the trigger.

Why Is It Gaining Steam Now?

Mr Trump became a catalyst for the protest Friday when he said during a campaign rally in Alabama that he wished that NFL players would be fired for kneeling during the national anthem.

"Wouldn't you love to see one of these NFL owners, when somebody disrespects our flag, to say, 'Get that son of a b**** off the field right now, out, he's fired. He's fired,'" Mr Trump said. "You know, some owner is going to do that. He's going to say, 'That guy that disrespects our flag, he's fired.' And that owner, they don't know it [but] they'll be the most popular person in this country."

Who Is Protesting?

Some football teams chose not to come out onto the field at all after Mr Trump's comments, while other teams have allowed their players to protest at their own discretion. In addition to most, if not all, of the NFL teams seeing some players protesting this weekend, baseball professionals and basketball professionals have joined in.

Notably, Patriots quarterback Tom Brady called Mr Trump's comments "divisive," and locked arms with his teammates during his game Sunday. Brady has remained mostly silent about Mr Trump, whom he has called a friend in the past.

Why Exactly Is This Such a Big Deal for People?

Mr Trump charges that kneeling during the national anthem is disrespectful to American servicemen and women, as do many of his supporters. The White House has repeatedly attempted to rebrand the protest as a protest of the American flag instead of against police brutality and racism in the US.

After Kaepernick first started the protest last year, he was criticised for introducing politics into sports. Many said that football was somehow sacrosanct, and that it should be a place where people can rise above politics.

But Is It Abnormal for Sports Stars to Make Their Political Opinions Known During Events?

No, not really. There's a pretty rich history of American sports stars wading into the political sphere.

For instance, John Carlos and Tommie Smith made headlines across the world when they raised the black power salute on the podium after winning in the 1968 Olympics. That protest brought them death threats, and they were expelled from the games.

Muhammad Ali is perhaps one of the best known American athletes to take a major political stand. While not a direct stand against racism, Ali refused to be drafted into the Vietnam War—a refusal that involved jail time. He did so on the basis of his faith, he said, but did note the cruel irony of asking black men to fight in Vietnam for a country that has treated them as subhuman.

More recently, NBA players like LeBron James, Kobe Bryant, and others, helped the Black Lives Matter movement pick up steam by wearing supportive shirts following the death of Eric Garner, who was choked to death in New York.

What Is the New NFL Rule?

NFL owners unanimously approved the new national anthem policy this week, requiring players to stand if they are on the field during the performance of the song. Players have the option to remain in the locker room during the anthem if they prefer.

If a player or other employee of a team kneels or sits during the anthem, the teams themselves are fined. The teams then have the option to fine the individual players or personnel for the infraction.

The vote was unanimous, but the owner of the San Francisco 49ers—the team Kaepernick played for when he started the protest—abstained from the vote.

The rule will be added to the NFLs game operations manual, and therefore will not be subject to collective bargaining. The NFL Players Association has said it will review the policy and "challenge any aspect" of the rule that violates the collective bargaining agreement between players and their employers.

What Has Happened to Kaepernick?

Kaepernick is not currently on any NFL team, even though many of his supporters argue that he is good enough to be picked up by a team. He said himself last year that he was ready to play if any team was willing to hire him.

But, while Kaepernick is out of an NFL job, he has remained busy with charity work. That includes a $1m pledge he made to charitable organisations, which has included support for a variety of groups. Kaepernick has largely refused to comment on the most recent NFL protests, and has refrained from responding to Mr Trump's criticism of the protest movement he started as "unpatriotic."

Periodical and Internet Sources Bibliography

The following articles have been selected to supplement the diverse views presented in this chapter.

Peggy Drexler, "When Role Models Fall: Talking to Boys About Heroes Gone Bad," *Huffington Post*, March 18, 2013. https:// www.huffingtonpost.com/peggy-drexler/when-role-models-fall -tal_b_2487190.html.

Lindsay Maxfield, "Charitable Athletes Give, but Just How Much?," KSL.com, March 7, 2013. https://www.ksl.com/?sid=24320788.

Ian Mendes, "Why Athletes Should Never Be Role Models for Kids," *Today's Parent*, September 19, 2014. https://www.todaysparent .com/blogs/athletes-never-be-role-models-for-kids/.

Vincent Pena, "Taking a Stand by Kneeling: An Analysis of National Anthem Protest Coverage," University of Nebraska, August 2017. https://digitalcommons.unl.edu/cgi/viewcontent .cgi?article=1056&context=journalismdiss://www.ksl .com/?sid=24320788.

Leigh Steinberg, "Why Do We Make Athletes Role Models?," *Forbes*, January 20, 2013. https://www.forbes.com/sites /leighsteinberg/2013/01/20/why-do-we-make-athletes-role -models/#7df6f61b6c34.

Tylt, "Do Rich Athletes Have a Responsibility to Donate More to Charity?," 2016. https://thetylt.com/sports/athletes-community -service-nba-nfl-nhl-mlb.

Universal Life Church Monastery, "Christian University Forces Athletes to Stand for National Anthem," October 2, 2017. https:// www.themonastery.org/blog/2017/10/christian-university-forces -athletes-to-stand-for-national-anthem/.

Richard Valdemar, "Gangsterish Athletes and Their Entourages," *Police: The Law Enforcement Magazine*, July 9, 2013. http://www .policemag.com/blog/gangs/story/2013/07/celebrity-gangsters .aspx.

OPPOSING
VIEWPOINTS®
SERIES

CHAPTER 2

Are Athletes Paid Fairly?

Chapter Preface

It seems nonsensical and unfair that the athletes who bring in billions of dollars of revenue for their college football and basketball programs earn zilch for their efforts while athletes just a few years older earn millions of dollars for playing professional sports. But that is reality.

Of course, most college athletes earn free rides to their universities and don't pay a penny for their educations. But that money is a drop in the bucket compared to what they make when one hundred thousand fans fill the stands every Saturday and purchase all that beer and all those hot dogs. Many have asked why those who toil, sweat, and display their vast talents on the college gridirons and hardwoods throughout America gain no financial benefit aside from a free education they might not even want.

Professional athletes make exorbitant salaries—even the minimum salaries approach $1 million a year. The best of the best earn up to $40 million annually. Critics question the fairness of such an economic arrangement while schoolteachers throughout the United States have taken to the streets to fight for livable wages. But this is a market-driven economy. Has anyone complained when a movie studio pays Tom Cruise millions to act in one picture?

Those who take a more moral outlook rail against college athletes making nothing and professional athletes making millions a year. Those who examine the high salaries of pros in a more practical way and take into consideration the capitalist system state that hundreds of millions of fans do not pay hundreds of dollars to listen to teachers teach, but they do to watch athletes perform. And therein lies the debate. It is the moral versus the practical.

> *"It was frustrating to win championship after championship every year, hear thousands chant my name, and then go to my bedroom to count my change so I could buy a burger."*

Rich College Programs Need to Pay Their Athletes

Kareem Abdul-Jabbar

In the following viewpoint, Kareem Abdul-Jabbar argues that the long-standing National Collegiate Athletic Association (NCAA) policy of providing athletes only scholarships is grossly unfair. College athletes do not earn money for the talents and efforts they provide—talents that result in billions of dollars in revenue for the school and team. Yet many struggle financially throughout their college careers. The author believes that, no matter how the rules are changed, college athletes deserve to be paid. Abdul-Jabar played in the National Basketball Association (NBA) for twenty seasons and is widely considered to be the greatest basketball player of all time.

"It's Time to Pay the Tab for America's College Athletes," by Kareem Abdul-Jabbar, Guardian News and Media Limited, January 9, 2018. Reprinted by permission.

As you read, consider the following questions:

1. What arguments does the author use to state his case that college athletes in money-making sports should be paid?
2. Does the author's status as a basketball icon give his views added validity?
3. How does Abdul-Jabbar connect his own experiences at the University of California–Los Angeles (UCLA) with his argument?

I n Thailand, bony little boys as young as nine and 10 are thrown into the boxing ring to punch each other into bloody submission while parents, relatives and other screaming adults bet on the outcome. Youth sports or child abuse? While most Americans feel outrage and revulsion at the idea, as a culture we are just as willing to toss our college-age kids into the gladiatorial arena to risk life and limb while we snack, guzzle and wager on the outcome. All while compensating the young athletes who are at risk with—relative to the money being made by sports barons—about the same as little kids we used to send into coal mines earned: a few coins and lots of chronic ailments. Sound too social justice warrior hyperbolic? During the three weeks of March Madness basketball last year, the NCAA earned $900m dollars while $9.2bn was gambled on the outcome. The players banging it out on the courts earned zip. Nada. Nothing.

I've been writing about this issue for several years now calling for college athletes to be paid the wages that they deserve and am sad to acknowledge that very little has changed since I was a college athlete at UCLA, so poor that I and most of my teammates could barely scrape by. But just as with every injustice, wrongs don't get righted unless we keep raising our voices again and again. So, once more unto the breach, dear friends, once more.

For those of you who think the life of a college athlete is all glitter and glamour, you couldn't be more wrong. If you came to college from a family with money then you were fine, but if you came on an athletic scholarship from blue-collar working families, then it was tough going. It wasn't hairshirts and gruel, but it wasn't nightly yacht parties and frat keggers either. It was mostly holing up in the dorms at night because you couldn't afford to go out and you needed a lot of rest after punishing practices. There's nothing wrong with living lean as a college student: it keeps you focused on your studies and teaches you discipline and the joys of being frugal. However, athletes must focus on their studies while also working a more than full-time job in the gym.

Playing basketball at UCLA was a seven-days-a-week job, involving intense practices, learning new plays, playing home games, and traveling around the country to compete against other schools. Our efforts earned millions of dollars for the university, both in cash and in recruiting advertisement to attract new students. But I was generally too poor to do anything but study, practice and play. The little spending money I managed to scrape together was earned on summer jobs. That money had to get me through the whole academic year. It was frustrating to win championship after championship every year, hear thousands chant my name, and then go to my bedroom to count my change so I could buy a burger.

What made it even worse was that students with academic scholarships were allowed to work jobs during the school year while we were forbidden to. And if we were injured seriously enough that we couldn't play anymore, our scholarships were revoked, despite the medical bills adding up. We were only as valuable as our ability to tote that ball and lift that score. Our coach, John Wooden, was sympathetic, but he made it clear that the NCAA would not change their policies. They were, he said, "immovable, like the sun rising in the east."

Here we are nearly 50 years later and the arguments for and against haven't changed. Portland Trailblazer Shabazz Napier described his experience as a college point guard in 2014 that was eerily, and sadly, so close to mine: "We do have hungry nights that we don't have enough money to get food in … Sometimes, there's hungry nights where I'm not able to eat, but I still gotta play up to my capabilities." The only thing that has significantly changed is that the NCAA, television broadcasters, and the colleges and universities are making a lot more money.

Top college coaches make between $4m and $9m per year, plus outside fees. In 40 out of the 50 states, they are the highest paid state employees. Of course, coaches in less profitable sports, such as baseball, make far less. And only a third of Division I men's basketball programs are profitable. These facts are tossed in our faces like sand to blind us to the awareness that other programs, like football at the University of Texas made $92m in profit in 2015, making it more profitable than most NFL teams. Yet, their players made nothing. Some apologists claim that the value of the scholarships, training, and other considerations give the players $50,000 to $125,000 a year in value, if not in cash. Plus, the best players get the invaluable publicity that they can cash in for big bucks when they turn pro. I certainly benefited from it. However, the reality is that, the chance of turning pro after college is less than 2% (except in baseball, which it's 11.6%).

Race is definitely a factor in determining which side people support. A 2017 HuffPost/YouGov survey showed only 27% of whites strongly or somewhat are for paying college athletes. However, 52% of African-Americans strongly or somewhat support paying. Why the divide along racial lines? A study in *Political Research Quarterly* concluded that "harboring negative racial views about blacks was the single strongest predictor of white opposition to paying athletes." There are other divides: men support paying college athletes more than women do, Democrats more than Republicans, adults under 30 more than adults 65 and older. But race is the largest percentage difference.

There are two reasons for this difference of opinion along racial lines. First, in basketball and football, which generate the most income, a large percentage of players at Division I schools are black. Their families, and the rest of the African-American community, don't want to continue the same policies of having their efforts exploited while others profit. Second, white Americans who don't have the same financial pressures think that receiving a sports scholarship is enough reward. Grand Valley State University professor Louis Moore, who studies African-American and sports history, observed, "In a sense, most whites see the black athlete and his presence in college as a gift. [He is] somehow getting a favor, and this is somehow not work." But scholarships depend on one's ability to play and they may be taken away in cases of severe injury. This leaves the student without the ability to play or earn an education.

The short list of opposition reasons would not stand up in any college logic class. They are startlingly similar to reasons not to pay minimum wages, not to have unions, not to ratify the women's vote, and on and on. But those shaking their Cheetos-stained fists at the prospect of paying college athletes don't care about the "elitist" rules of logic, they care about the profitable rules of bottom line or their blind allegiance to outdated tradition. As my old pal Henry V might say today, "Once more unto the breach, dear friends, once more; / Or close the wall up with our fallen, failed, or foresaken college athletes."

Or maybe we should just set out a tip jar.

> "*Alipate testified that 'one of the things that helps the entire student body rally around the football team is the fact that the players on the football team are also students.'*"

The NCAA Argues for Amateurism
Jon Solomon

In the following viewpoint, Jon Solomon reports that the National Collegiate Athletic Association (NCAA) vigorously defended its policy of maintaining amateurism among its athletes. The organization, which has been strongly criticized in recent years for perceived hypocrisy and inconsistent enforcement issues, has also been disparaged for its continued refusal to pay college athletes, who earn extraodinary amounts of money for their universities. Solomon notes that the NCAA sent a wide variety of so-called experts to testify in favor of its stand that football and basketball players should not even be compensated for their likenesses being used to attract business. Solomon is a former enterprise reporter for the Birmingham News.

"Should College Players Be Paid? NCAA Files Vigorous Defense of Amateurism Through Leaders' Words," by Jon Solomon, Alabama Media Group, December 13, 2013. Reprinted by permission.

As you read, consider the following questions:

1. Does the author indicate any bias for either side in this viewpoint?

2. Whose testimony as reported by the author resonates the strongest in arguing for maintaining amateurism among college athletes?

3. Does the threat that schools would be forced to cut certain sports to pay players hold water?

The NCAA filed a motion for summary judgment this week in the Ed O'Bannon case and staged a vigorous defense of its amateurism model. Numerous presidents, chancellors, athletics directors, commissioners and even players are cited in the motion defending the model and outlining what they describe as dire consequences if football and men's basketball players are compensated for use of their name, image and likeness.

The filing details the NCAA's five procompetitive arguments for not allowing players to be paid: amateurism, competitive balance, integrating educating and athletics, viability of other sports, and increased output for participation and games for the public to enjoy. The O'Bannon plaintiffs previously sought an injunction to end the NCAA's restraint against compensating athletes for commercial use.

Mostly, the NCAA motion reveals a united front against the so-called "pay for play" model over the licensing of athletes' name, image and likeness in the multi-billion-dollar college sports industry. Leaders at major universities, including Texas and Michigan, testified that they might have to cut sports if the plaintiffs realized their goal of evenly dividing television revenue with players. Suggestions were made that rivalries and national competitions could end.

SEC Commissioner Mike Slive entered the case for the first time and testified that paying players would "significantly disrupt the competitive balance" within the SEC and other conferences. He said sharing half of broadcast revenue with players "would have a disproportionate effect on institutions in the SEC and elsewhere with smaller athletic budgets where the broadcast revenues make up a larger percentage of their overall budget."

Similar statements are made throughout the hundreds of pages of documents filed by the NCAA. The NCAA also attempts to show that no other amateur sport appears to allocate any broadcast revenue to players for use of their names, images and likenesses, and that paying players would make college sports less popular. The O'Bannon plaintiffs previously cited how licensing revenue is shared in professional sports leagues.

The O'Bannon plaintiffs claimed last month they are "not advocating for an end to the principle of amateurism, nor are they advocating salaries." The plaintiffs said the NCAA hasn't proven that college sports are popular because of the NCAA's amateurism definition, or that the popularity would decrease if athletes were paid for commercial use of their names, images and likenesses.

Lauren Stiroh, an expert for the NCAA, wrote in a report that even the Olympics, which allows athletes to be paid, do not appear to allocate any broadcast revenue to the players for use of their name, image and likeness.

Former CBS Sports President Neal Pilson, an expert for the NCAA, cited the US Golf Association, televised high school sports games, the Little League World Series and the Olympics as examples of amateur sports in which athletes are not paid based solely for appearing on TV.

Pilson, who is now a television consultant for conferences, wrote that he believes paying college athletes, as described in either model brought forth by the O'Bannon plaintiffs, "would undermine the key features of college sports that make them tremendously popular even though they exhibit an inferior quality of play and therefore would pose a significant risk of jeopardizing the popularity of college sports."

The NCAA cites an expert report by Michael Dennis from a survey of 2,455 people in which 68.9 percent were "opposed to paying money to student-athletes on college football and men's college basketball teams in addition to covering their college expenses."

The NCAA also cited a statement from economist Roger Noll, an expert for the plaintiffs, who testified that "probably there is a number at which, if college athletes are paid that amount, it would negatively impact the popularity of the sport."

Would Schools Cut Sports by Paying Players?

The heart of the NCAA's motion for summary judgment is statements from commissioners, presidents, chancellors, athletics directors and even players from around the country. The NCAA attempts to show the value of integrating academics with athletics without paying players—and the threatened consequences if payments occur.

Wake Forest President Nathan Hatch testified that paying broadcast money to players would "reduce the ability of Wake Forest to compete successfully in football and men's basketball. It would be more difficult for Wake Forest to recruit student-athletes who would otherwise be interested in the unique education and campus environment we offer."

Michigan State Athletics Director Mark Hollis testified that rival Michigan already generates $140 million in revenue, compared to $90 million for Michigan State. Given Michigan State's lower revenue base, "if Michigan State had to pay $10 million in broadcast revenue to football and men's basketball student-athletes, Michigan State would have to choose between continuing to recruit the most elite student-athletes and cutting opportunities for student-athletes in other sports," Hollis said. "Based on my experience, the same would be true for most of the other universities in The Big Ten."

Pac-12 Commissioner Larry Scott testified that "it is far from clear" that making payments to only male athletes would be permissible under Title IX law. Even if it was permitted, doing so "would run counter to the enormous strides that have been made" in athletic participation by females, Scott said.

University of Wisconsin Chancellor Rebecca Blank said that if Wisconsin had to share 50 percent of television revenue with players, the university would respect gender equity but athletic opportunities at the university would "shrink substantially."

Big 12 Commissioner Bob Bowlsby said television revenue sharing would likely discontinue some programs in the Big 12, "especially at universities in rural areas."

Oklahoma Athletics Joe Castiglione testified: "I understand that plaintiffs have argued that any shortfall created by paying broadcast revenue to the football and men's basketball players could be offset by reductions in coaching salaries and expenditures on facilities. Based on my experience over the past several decades in intercollegiate athletics, I disagree."

The NCAA argues that the competitive balance would significantly change if athletes were allowed to be paid for use of their name, image and likeness. The O'Bannon plaintiffs have argued high-revenue teams already have a significant recruiting edge.

"If athletes were paid for the use of their name, image and likeness, the schools that were able to pay the most money would get the best athletes," Conference USA Commissioner Britton Banowsky testified. "This would give those schools a significant (and unfair) advantage in recruiting and would reduce the competitive balance across schools both within my conference and across other conferences."

If each school plays by different rules, "fair competition would be eroded," said Michigan President Mary Sue Coleman, "causing ultimately the disintegration of rivalries and national competitions like March Madness."

Texas Women's Athletics Director Christine Plonsky testified that even if payments were negotiated prior to athletes participating in a season and paid after graduation, "allowing the student to negotiate with the university for a percentage of the school's broadcast revenue would change college athletics from an amateurism model in which the student-athlete is first and foremost a student to a model in which money drives athletics decision making."

Plonsky said college sports would be on "dangerous ground" by encouraging additional "entitlement thinking" among young people "who have an opportunity to take an admission slot on our campuses."

"We don't apologize for the system," Plonsky said. "The system is rigorous, the system is tough, they're held to higher standards, they're on accelerated degree tracks in order to maintain eligibility. We can list for you many reasons why it's not for everybody, but if you choose to engage in it, we will support you in it, but it is what it is. And pay-for-play, in my opinion will never happen and shouldn't happen, because it will absolutely skew the meaningful core values that the NCAA's strategic plan and our strategic plan for our athletics program espoused."

Would College Sports Be Less Popular by Paying Players?

Michigan Athletics Director Dave Brandon testified that paying athletes for appearing on television would "fundamentally change" the relationship between fans and players and cause problems similar to professional sports when a player has a bad season.

"We don't cut or trade student-athletes who underperform," Brandon said. "We support them and continue to provide the same benefits and services whether they are star players or never leave the bench. However, if U-M student-athletes were paid, it would dramatically increase the amount of pressure on those student-athletes to perform. Fans would equate their investment in ticket prices, donation, etc. to 'paying for performance,' and if the performance isn't there, fans would more quickly react in a similar fashion to what we see in professional sports."

Coleman, Michigan's president, argued that "amateurism is fundamental to athletics at Michigan and sports competition throughout the nation. Amateurism is not broken; it is essential

… A musician could choose to attend Julliard and focus exclusively on music, just as a talented football player could choose to play Arena Football."

Instead, Coleman said, talented students attend Michigan for the "integrated experience." She said Michigan fans delight in "watching true stories, often Cinderella stories, of kids playing their heart out on the field while also working hard in the classroom to get an education for their future." She cited a recent "inspiring speech" by Michigan offensive lineman Quinton Washington at a team football banquet in which he explained that he used to have serious speech impediments but now has already graduated.

Bowlsby testified that universities sponsor athletics programs to promote their education mission—"to promote the name on the front of the jersey, as opposed to promoting the names of individuals on the backs of the jerseys. This is what makes collegiate athletics distinct from other forms of athletics."

Bowlsby said "there is no question" college football and men's basketball fans and alumni donors would respond negatively to players being paid to appear on television. Many fans and donors attended these colleges and "hearken back to collegiate athletics because of a yearning for the time they had on campus and the experience they had as students," Bowlsy testified. "Paying student-athletes separates the student-athlete from that experience, and alumni and fans would see them differently."

Bowlsby said paying athletes would change many athletes' motivation for being on campus. "It would shift the focus away from the role of athletes as students who are part of the university," he testified. "This would be untenable for institutions of higher education."

Blank, Wisconsin's chancellor, said that "fans follow college football because of the joy of seeing players with whom the fans identify. Fans cheer for student-athletes based in part on a perception that they are students playing for the love of the game, rather than professionals playing for payment.

"Based on my conversations and observations, paying football and men's basketball players would seriously degrade interest in college athletics and break the connection that many fans feel with the players. No doubt, some people would still remain loyal college football and basketball fans, but I would expect lower commitment to the team and less excitement about the game and the players."

Blank said paying players would send a message that the school "cares about and rewards performance on the field and not performance in the classroom. Other students are likely to view the football and men's basketball players differently if they are paid … It will be a loss to the student-athlete and his peers if he is seen, due to payment beyond his educational expenses, as a professional who is at the institution to play a sport, not get an education."

South Carolina President Harris Pastides testified that paying players a licensing fee for appearing on television would "negatively impact community spirit at those games … Fans of college football and men's basketball are loyal to and passionate about their team precisely because they believe they are cheering for students with USC uniforms on their backs that may have the opportunity to live [the] American dream of getting drafted one day in the future, but right now are going to class, getting an education, and are not yet corrupted by money and other financial influences."

Slive testified that fans watch games in order to cheer for their alma mater or due to a strong affiliation with a community. He said that "professionalizing college athletics by paying salaries or similar compensation to student athletes would negatively change this environment and the relationship between student-athletes and their university by putting too much emphasis on individuals, and thereby distorting their experience as students of their university."

Big Ten Commissioner Jim Delany testified that even deferred payments to players after their eligibility expires "would send the message to student-athletes that they are in college to maximize their commercial opportunities rather than to maximize their educational opportunities—exactly the opposite of the message The Big Ten has tried to send for over 100 years."

Delany said at least some players' focus would shift away from their academic work. "If there were tens or hundreds of thousands of dollars being offered to those students to appear in televised games, I am concerned that athletics would become primary and the whole attempt to achieve a balance of academics and athletics would become more difficult," Delany said.

The NCAA's motion cites favorable excerpts from depositions by some current football players—Moses Alipate of Minnesota, Chase Garnham of Vanderbilt, Darius Robinson of Clemson and Jake Fischer of Arizona—who joined the case as plaintiffs in July.

Alipate testified that "one of the things that helps the entire student body rally around the football team is the fact that the players on the football team are also students." Robinson said fans were "more engaged with the players [in college sports] as far as seeing us around and things like that."

Fischer said he thinks the majority of his football teammates "take school seriously" and "came to school both for football and for an education." Garnham said he came to Vanderbilt because he wanted to compete in the SEC and get a great education.

A motion hearing is scheduled for February. The case, which was partially certified as a class action by a federal judge last month, is scheduled for trial next June.

US District Judge Claudia Wilken previously denied the plaintiffs' collective attempt to seek $3.2 billion in damages from 2005–06 through 2010–11, but allowed them to attempt to share licensing revenue moving forward. The plaintiffs have suggested they will appeal her denial to not certify the class over past damages.

"Right now, we're not having any settlement talks," NCAA President Mark Emmert said Wednesday at the IMG Intercollegiate Athletics Forum. "If their goal is to move toward a pay-for-play model, which is what it seems to be, there's not consideration of that at all."

> *"Athletes should actively pursue internships, faculty-mentoring and career shadowing opportunities as they are precursors to career readiness."*

Student Athletes Must Make Academics a Priority

Kimberly S. Miloch and Michelle Buggs

In the following viewpoint, Kimberly S. Miloch and Michelle Buggs argue that college athletes should be realistic about their chances of having a successful career as a professional athlete. Since so few student athletes actually make it all the way to lucrative careers in professional athletics, the authors stress the importance of preparing for an alternate career. Unfortunately, many universities fail at preparing their top athletes academically in the interest of allowing them to focus on their sport. This does the athletes a great disservice later in life. Miloch is a professor of sport management at Texas Woman's University. Buggs is director of undergraduate programs at Texas Woman's University.

As you read, consider the following questions:

1. Athletes from which university are suing the school and the NCAA?
2. What percentage of college football players will get a contract in the NFL?
3. Why are NCAA rules confusing, according to the viewpoint?

T he fanfare over the 2015 National Football League (NFL) Draft in Chicago can trick one into believing that playing college sports is a ticket to a professional career and a multimillion dollar payday.

But we know it isn't.

The reality is that few college football players will be drafted and the overwhelming majority of student athletes will need to go into careers other than professional sports.

To ensure a career other than professional sports, student athletes need to take responsibility for their academic lives.

An ongoing case at the University of North Carolina (UNC)– Chapel Hill, in which student athletes are suing the National Collegiate Athletic Association (NCAA) and the university in a class action lawsuit illustrates how things can go wrong when student athletes do not pay attention to their own education.

Based on our experience, we believe student athletes need to play a more proactive role. One of us (Kimberly S Miloch) competed as a student athlete and subsequently worked with the United States Tennis Association (USTA). The other author (Michelle Buggs), mentored college students at all levels for more than ten years and has extensive experience in both student and academic affairs.

Few Student Athletes Get Lucrative Jobs

Data illustrate that professional sport careers are unlikely for football players and the vast majority of college athletes. Fewer than four percent of football players will go on to play professionally.

The NCAA estimates that of the 71,000 athletes who currently play college football, only 15,842 are eligible for 256 draft spots this weekend.

Of these, fewer than two percent will secure a contract with an NFL League team.

Some of those not drafted by the NFL may be able to pursue positions with teams in the Canadian Football League (CFL) or the Arena League (AFL) but even considering these leagues, fewer than four percent will play professionally.

This pattern holds true for the majority of college athletes in all sports. Only about one percent will be playing in the National Basketball Association (NBA) and Women's National Basketball Association (WNBA), almost nine percent in Major League Baseball, just under seven percent in the National Hockey League (NHL) and just over one percent in Major League Soccer (MLS).

Despite these numbers, many student athletes do not pay attention to their academic lives. Often, they rely too heavily on the NCAA or coaches and administrators to chart their academic path.

Academic Dishonesty

And this lapse, in part, is what led to the situation and the systemic cheating at UNC.

The "courses" that these student athletes took included independent studies in which they wrote papers assigned and graded by non-faculty staff with no expertise on the topic.

The staff member assigned As and high Bs and later enrolled athletes in lecture courses managed like independent studies. The courses were not taught by faculty nor did the athletes attend lectures. No instruction was provided in these courses.

UNC has claimed not to have been aware of the situation. And the NCAA has refused to take responsibility for monitoring the quality of academics at an institution.

This is in contrast to the NCAA mission and core values and what has been stated previously in legal proceedings, and various official publications.

While we agree that the NCAA and its member institutions should take responsibility for the quality of athletes' education, we also believe student athletes should be proactive and work in tandem with their university and the NCAA to ensure a meaningful education.

Students Confused About Rules

In its role of overseeing college athletics, the NCAA has rules to support athletes' academic life. Athletic departments across the country provide athlete support services and consistently monitor compliance with all NCAA rules and regulations.

Examples of such support include athletic department advisors for student athletes, formalized tutoring services, mandatory study halls and departmental monitoring of athlete attendance and grades.

College degree plans are increasingly refined and progress toward degree is regularly reported to the NCAA.

These rules can be confusing, as we know through experience. Having been athletes in high school and college and now academic administrators, we remember numerous conversations with teammates and other athletes trying to understand NCAA rules.

Each fall we would have a session with athletic administrators who briefed us on expectations for compliance and standards of conduct. These sessions were confusing. And this was well before the digital age and social media.

We understand that many student athletes may not be fully aware of the NCAA rules or even pay attention them. This is because they do not fully realize the value of their education.

However, we want to emphasize the importance of student athletes remaining vigilant in order to prevent cases like the UNC incident from happening again. Student athletes must ensure that lecture courses do indeed include lectures and are taught by qualified faculty or expert instructors.

Additionally, athletes should understand that formal instruction should be provided with any course, including independent studies. When this is not the case, athletes should address it with an academic advisor or an administrator, such as a dean of students.

Pay Attention to Academic Life

Incidents of academic fraud in college athletics are not new. College-athletes cannot rely on the NCAA or their respective institution to be a watchdog. In past instances, breaches in academic integrity have occurred when athletes have submitted assignments written by someone else or when other individuals have taken tests on behalf of athletes.

The outcome of the UNC case could have far reaching impact and could lead to significant reforms, particularly at Football Bowl Subdivision institutions. The NCAA is on the hook, too, but not more than the athletes who are accountable to themselves.

The American Association of Colleges and Universities emphasizes personal and social responsibility as a core commitment of higher education.

Athletes should actively pursue internships, faculty-mentoring and career shadowing opportunities as they are precursors to career readiness.

Student athletes should realize their integrity and education is at stake when they allow such situations like the UNC scandal to occur. They must work together and hold one another accountable for earning a meaningful education.

If student athletes don't want to warm the bench in the game of life, they must pursue their academic career with as much intensity as they pursue a conference or national championship, and they should do so in tandem with their institution and the NCAA.

> *"It is the very fans who often grumble about the 'ridiculous' wages paid to top athletes who in effect set their salaries."*

The Fans Are to Blame for Athletes' Salaries

Gene Callahan

In the following viewpoint, Gene Callahan argues that in our market-driven economy, it is fans as consumers who in effect set player salaries. Fans show their financial support by buying team merchandise and stadium tickets and by watching the games on cable TV. These actions tell team owners that the players are worth the salaries they make. The author concludes that everything depends on society's priorities; if people decide to spend their money on things other than sports and entertainment, they are free to do so. Callahan is a writer and economist who teaches at the State University of New York at Purchase.

As you read, consider the following questions:

1. What former New York Yankee is used as an example of an athlete pulling in an exorbitant salary?
2. What is consumer sovereignty?
3. What point does the author make by comparing Britney Spears to Bach?

I was sitting in a sports bar recently when the bartender and three of the patrons near me began discussing the salary of New York Yankee third-baseman Alex Rodriguez. (Rodriguez currently makes roughly $25 million per season.) One of the customers said it was absurd that Rodriguez makes so much when, for instance, teachers, charged with educating our children make only $50,000 or $60,000 per year. The bartender defended Rodriguez's salary, asking, "If someone offered you $25 million, would you turn them down? And besides, if the owners can pay ballplayers that much, how much are they making?" (His second defense of Rodriguez's income level is, of course, open to the objection that the owners are even more overpaid than are players.)

I am presenting an account of their conversation here not because I suspect that the readers of *The Freeman* are especially interested in Rodriguez, but because it struck me as representative of a type of complaint commonly made about the workings of the market: To many people it just doesn't seem right that pop stars/investment bankers/athletes get paid so much more than nurses/firemen/teachers.

What no one participating in the barroom banter that afternoon seemed to consider was the question of just who is responsible for the size of Rodriguez's salary. The correct answer, especially given that we were in a sports bar, is that the discussants themselves ultimately are the ones setting such high rewards for being an outstanding athlete. (Not just the four of them, of course, but them in concert with all other sports fans.)

It is the very fans who often grumble about the "ridiculous" wages paid to top athletes who in effect set their salaries. That's because in a market economy the price paid for any factor of production (including labor services) arises from the choices consumers make about the items they wish to buy and how much they are willing to pay. Producers face costs in providing a good, and if they estimate that buyers will not pay at least enough for their output to cover their costs plus some profit, the good will not be produced. Those estimates can turn out to be over-optimistic:

producers are often mistaken in gauging consumer demand, and many a business has gone under because it spent more to manufacture its offerings than consumers were willing to pay. But competition among entrepreneurs for buyers' dollars rewards those entrepreneurs whose forecasts are generally most accurate with profits that allow them to remain in business and invest even more in the future.

Consumers must bid enough to prompt producers into action, and the price of every good—industrial products as well as consumption items—can be traced to consumer choice. Producers of items needed for the production of consumer goods will find it rewarding to produce those items only if consumers value the final goods enough to pay for the resources and work necessary to create them.

What's more, the costs producers face in their operations are not determined by nonhuman factors such as energy expenditures, chemical transformations, or the abundance or scarcity of various raw materials; rather they are the consequence of the producers' evaluation of alternative ways in which they might earn their livings by meeting consumer demand. Of course, producers must not ignore physical reality in their business decisions: it will clearly require far more time and energy to manufacture skillets from iron mined on Mars than from the same metal mined on earth. However, unless consumers value "Martian skillets" more than the terrestrial variety, expending all that effort to procure otherworldly metal will not result in a higher price being paid for it. It is the preferences of consumers that drive the formation of prices all the way backwards along the production chain. If some resource could be used in the creation of a consumer good, but producers judge that their efforts to acquire it will not add enough to the value of the final product to be worth their while, they simply will choose not to employ it; they have no power to drive up the price of the end product by picking an extravagant way of manufacturing it.

This aspect of the market economy, which has been termed "consumer sovereignty," is entirely independent of how concerned a proprietor is about the welfare of his customers. One entrepreneur may start a firm because of a sincere conviction that the product or service he plans to provide will bring immense benefits to his clientele. Another may be motivated solely by his desire to become fabulously wealthy. But to succeed, both will be equally bound to judge accurately as to how much consumers will value his offerings. Certainly, an unscrupulous businessman may try to deceive consumers about the true nature of what he is selling, but that is more accurately classified as theft rather than commerce and properly is subject to legal sanctions.

Often the understanding of consumer sovereignty as presented above is attacked for not taking into account the character flaws and cognitive shortcomings of the flesh-and-blood people who really populate any economy. However, asserting that in a free market the consumers are sovereign in no way implies that every decision they make about spending their money is perfect and immune to moral or prudential criticism. If a father bets extravagantly on horseraces while neglecting to provide adequately for his children's needs for food, clothing, shelter, and education, then his friends and family are quite justified in reproving his conduct, and if the neglect is severe, legal remedies may be appropriate. If a wealthy heiress spends her inheritance entirely on lavish evenings of debauchery, then a newspaper's society columnist is perfectly entitled to bemoan that she is not putting her fortune to a better use. And while it is not immoral if I buy apples for $10 a bag despite their being available for $5 just down the street, a friend may sensibly and helpfully point out that I am needlessly wasting my money.

The recognition that, in the market, the consumer is the ultimate boss does not rely on any idealized model of him as a perfectly rational, fully informed, utility-maximizing supercomputer, whose choices are beyond reproach and are incapable of being improved on through reasoned consideration.

Some critics of "consumerism" argue that, in today's market societies, consumers' choices about what to purchase are "not really free" because they have been unduly shaped by massive and

ATHLETES DESERVE A PIECE OF THE PIE

In 2011, Philadelphia Eagles quarterback Michael Vick is scheduled to make anywhere between $16 and $20 million on a one-year contract in the National Football League, meaning he is in line to receive a little over $1 million for each regular season game he plays this season (assuming the league lockout comes to an end). Years ago, a salary like Vick's would have been considered outrageously high, but in today's world of professional sports, hefty, big-money deals are common. The growing frequency of large sports salaries has not exactly garnered the approval of the public, however, and many believe athletes are being overpaid, receiving ridiculous amounts of money to entertain. In spite of the criticism, high salaries are clearly not ruining the games in which the wealthy players participate.

Sherman Howard, a former running back for the Bears, recently told the *Chicago Tribune* newspaper that the current generation of NFL players "think finances is the main thing" and care about little else. And while there are ongoing negotiations to refine the league's restrictions on rookie contracts as a result of first-year players signing for loads of guaranteed money before ever setting foot

pervasive marketing efforts designed to convince people that they want or even need products that they could easily forgo, some of which actually diminish their quality of life. A paradigmatic case is cigarettes: smokers are persuaded to buy them because tobacco companies have made them seem glamorous or sources of great pleasure, but in reality they ruin the health of smokers, who will come to regret their habit.

Not Immune from Error

It is true that consumers are no less immune from error in their choices of what to buy than are producers in their choice of what to make. But if we are to allow free speech and treat our fellow citizens as autonomous individuals responsible for and entitled on a field, professional sports as a whole have not been damaged by the increase in revenue for athletes. In fact, it would be quite an understatement to suggest the NFL, among other pro sports organizations, have been ruined by high player salaries. A 2009 poll among sports fans indicated a 10-percent increase of followers for both football and baseball over the last few decades, while teams rake in hundreds of millions of dollars per year, largely because of the income generated from fan-purchased items such as game tickets and merchandise–most of which is bought to watch or show support for certain players.

Just because professional sports players generally have high salaries does not mean they are not entitled to their earnings. In America, the ultimate goal of people is usually to find prosperity and success, so it is not justifiable to say athletes should not be able to make tons of money for playing games if that is what they set out to achieve. The US is enthralled with entertainment, and professional sports are a part of that market. Athletes simply carry out that type of entertainment and risk their careers and bodies to do so.

"Are High Athlete Salaries Ruining Professional Sports?" Cody Benjamin, May 31, 2011.

to make their own decisions, then it follows that they must be allowed to evaluate arguments as to how they should allocate their time and resources themselves. In a free society the proper remedy available to those who deplore smoking or are convinced that their fellows should buy fewer Britney Spears CDs and more Bach is to persuade others of their beliefs. That such efforts at persuasion will sometimes fail is an inescapable consequence of treating others as free agents rather than as one's vassals whose lives can be directed as one wills.

It is important to note than nothing argued here suggests that every salary we see today is the result of consumers' voluntary choices. To the extent that any interest group, such as corporate managers, can successfully lobby for favorable legal restrictions on free-market processes, such as laws hampering corporate takeovers, then the members of that group might be able to earn more than they would through purely voluntary transactions. Similarly, the owners of baseball teams who receive municipal subsidies to build fancy, new stadiums can pay their players more than they could without that government largess.

Nevertheless, the enormous salaries earned by sports stars are chiefly the result of the willingness of their fans to pay to see them play. If my neighbors in the sports bar are seriously distressed that star athletes make so much more than educators, the power to alter that situation lies with them. They can stop paying so much for ESPN and tickets to ballgames and instead spend the money they save on their children's schooling. I certainly would not complain about such a shift in people's priorities. But it is the only way a free people can address the situation.

> *"The majority of Americans not only rank spending on tickets for professional sports events ahead of spending on education for themselves and their children, but also likely will spend more dollars on athletics than education."*

Athletes' High Salaries Are a Good Sign for All of Us

William L. Anderson

In the following viewpoint, William L. Anderson argues that the explosive growth of athletes' salaries indicates that we have become more prosperous. While some may write it off as greed or faulty priorities, Anderson uses economic principles to conclude that superstar athletes' high salaries are appropriate because there are simply fewer successful pro athletes, as compared to more common professions like teachers and police officers. What's more, Anderson asserts that we should applaud the astronomical deals given to the top players because their high salaries are a reflection on the overall prosperity of our society. Anderson is an economics professor at Frostburg State University.

"In Praise of Athletes' High Salaries," by William L. Anderson, Foundation for Economic Education, August 1, 2000. https://fee.org/articles/in-praise-of-athletes-high-salaries/. Licensed under CC BY 4.0 International.

As you read, consider the following questions:

1. What relatively low-paying profession does the author contrast with professional athletes?
2. How many people receive PhDs in the United States each year?
3. What connection does the author draw between professional sports and our well-being?

While teaching in public schools many years ago, I found that almost all teachers believed they were underpaid and underappreciated. Things probably have not changed. My colleagues expressed their sentiments by hanging a newspaper editorial on a bulletin board in the teachers' lounge that condemned the high salaries of professional athletes.

"Americans do not value education," the editorial opined, citing as proof the fact that "a mediocre halfback in the NFL" was paid more than three times the average teacher's salary. The statement had its desired effect, judging from my colleagues' responses to the disgruntled editorial writer.

The message was clear: Americans have their priorities wrong. If they truly valued education more than professional sports, teachers would be paid more than professional athletes. People recoil at the high salaries players receive, salaries that seem to be out of kilter with what the rest of us earn. In an extreme example, Michael Jordan was paid $36 million to play his last season with the Chicago Bulls of the National Basketball Association. Even most medical doctors fail to earn such a sum during their entire working lives. That athletes are much better paid is prima facie evidence that people in this country have no appreciation for what is really important. Thus the state should force the right values on us.

Even while more and more Americans attend professional athletic events, the athletes and their sports are under greater attack. Furthermore, the off-field behavior of many athletes—including the commission of serious crimes in some well-publicized cases—

allegedly demonstrates that we should not be paying great sums of money to people who are not proper role models for our children.

Some of the details of the editorial are true. In fact, the gap between the average salaries for teachers and professional athletes in the last two decades has grown considerably. Yet, incredible as it may sound to the average person, this is a positive sign. Far from being an indication that people are worse off, the explosive growth in the salaries of professional athletes, as well as the overall surge of professional sports, demonstrates that individuals—including teachers—have become more prosperous.

Such a statement flies in the face of conventional understanding. After all, macroeconomic statistics like the consumer price index allegedly tell us that real incomes have fallen for the past three decades. Not only is it difficult to argue against such numbers, but for those of us who believe in limited government, there is also a dark satisfaction gained by showing that living standards are down as government intervention in the economy has increased.

The Power of Economic Analysis

The praxeological tools of economic analysis, however, are much more powerful than numbers created by the US Department of Labor, and while we would like to be arguing that the expansion of the state in recent years has meant an absolute decline in living standards, perhaps there is another case to be made. We should be telling the world that free-market capitalism has succeeded *despite* the ubiquitous intrusions of government.

To understand how the increases in the salaries of professional athletes demonstrate that all of us are better off, we turn to an old issue: the diamond-water paradox. In *The Wealth of Nations*, Adam Smith asked why a diamond could fetch much more money in the marketplace than could water, despite the fact that water was much more necessary for human existence.

The solution to the paradox came from the "marginalists" of the mid and late nineteenth century, including Carl Menger of Austria, William Stanley Jevons of England, and Jules Dupuit of France.

Value, they astutely pointed out, is determined by the usefulness of the marginal available unit of the item in question, or *marginal utility*. An individual imputes value to a particular *unit* of water, not to the overall characteristics of water itself.

Because water is plentiful and diamonds are scarce relative to water, in normal cases a unit of water will not be valued as highly as a diamond. However, if someone were wandering in the desert, dying of thirst, he might very well be willing to trade a beautifully cut diamond for a canteen full of water!

Diminishing Utility

Take a desert traveler who stumbles on an oasis. He pulls a bucket of water from a well and drinks to quench his thirst. After he has drunk to his fill, he uses the next bucket of water to fill his canteens, while the bucket after that goes to watering his pack animals. Each successive bucket is applied to lower valued uses.

We next apply this example to one's income. Assume that Joe is a teacher and is paid once a month. His first payments go to those things that are most essential to his well-being: rent (or house payment) and food, along with other bills that must be paid immediately. In other words, Joe applies his income in an ordinal fashion, going from his highest valued to his lowest valued priorities. It is only after those things that are essential to him receive payment that he can apply his leftover income to less important things like entertainment, eating out, and the like. The vast majority of people will spend their incomes as Joe does.

This brings us to spending on education versus spending on professional sports. If the editorial writer is correct, the majority of Americans not only rank spending on tickets for professional sports events ahead of spending on education for themselves and their children, but also likely will spend more dollars on athletics than education.

Even without resorting to a bevy of statistics, one can surmise that the conditions required to make the editorialist's statement true simply do not exist. Take public education, for example. The budgets of most state governments devote more than 50 percent of their funding to education. If one includes the added expenditures for private education, the numbers become enormous.

According to the 1999 *Statistical Abstracts of the United States*, total expenditures in 1995 on private and public education at all levels was $532.4 billion. In contrast, Americans spent $57.2 billion on movies (including video rentals) and $13.1 billion on commercial sports (including horseracing).

What's more, Americans on average spent approximately 10.7 percent of their 1995 income on education. This was not a radical departure: the share of income spent on education in 1980 was 10.1 percent. Comparing education payments to expenditures on other things, one finds that people spent more only on food ($690.5 billion), housing ($688.2 billion), and medical care ($766.2 billion).

Listing education spending has two drawbacks. First, since utility is ordinal and not cardinal, the numbers themselves do not measure utility; at best, they are a representation (or proxy). Second, most education expenditures come from taxes, which are not voluntary payments. However, since the critics whom we are answering have insinuated that Americans do not pay enough taxes for education in proportion to what they pay to see athletes, it is appropriate to list tax payments along with voluntary payments for private education.

Therefore, one cannot conclude from these numbers that Americans rank professional sports above education. However, how does one square the fact that many professional athletes make huge salaries while most teachers make about $40,000 a year? For example, in 1995 the average salary for a major league baseball player was $1.1 million, while the average pay for a player in the National Basketball Association was $1.9 million. The average salary for a National Football League player that year was "only" $714,000.

To most observers, the difference between the salaries for professional athletes and teachers seems to reflect mistaken priorities. However, to an economist this disparity is explained by the law of diminishing marginal utility.

More Teachers than Athletes

People who can qualify to be teachers are relatively more abundant than athletes who can withstand the rigors of professional sports. Furthermore, the professional athlete operates in an arena in which he (or she, as women's professional sports are increasing) can entertain large numbers of people at one time. For example, it is estimated that more than a billion people worldwide see the Super Bowl. The best lecturers may speak before a few hundred listeners, and most teachers teach 25 students or so at a time.

Each year more than 40,000 people receive Ph.D.s in the United States, while perhaps 40 rookies may make it into the NBA. For the few who do make it into the pros, their expected tenure is short, maybe a few years on average. A teacher, on the other hand, may be able to practice his profession for up to 40 years. Nor do most professional athletes strike it rich. The vast majority work in the obscurity of minor league sports or other relatively low-paid positions, such as a golf professional at a country club. In other words, the multimillionaire athlete is the great exception, not the rule.

If one can get past the feelings of envy regarding the highly paid but often publicly immature athletes, one sees that the only way for the escalation of high salaries to continue is for society as a whole to become wealthier. As noted, individuals generally put spending for sports events far down on their list of priorities.

That being the case, it is obvious that greater sums of money are poured into professional sports because people have increasing amounts of income left over after paying for their highest values. The pattern of sports salaries bears this out.

Babe Ruth made his highly publicized $80,000 a year in the late 1920s, an astounding salary at that time. However, even accounting for inflation, Ruth's salary today would hardly place him near the top of the baseball payroll. Even as recently as 1985, the average salary for a player in the NBA was just $325,000. If adjusted for inflation, that figure in constant dollars for 1997 would be $414,000. Yet, the average NBA salary in 1997 was $2.1 million.

Unless US society has undergone a sea change in preferences in the last 15 years, the pay increase for NBA players could have come about only because Americans had also gained in real income. Likewise, the proliferation of minor professional sports—like arena football—means that Americans have even more disposable income than before and can afford to pay to see such sports. Otherwise, these teams would drown in red ink and be out of business.

Such analysis most likely will not satisfy those social critics who believe unless government guides our every thought, we will always make bad decisions with our money. If one examines the spending patterns of most people, however, one finds that perhaps the fears that individuals have their priorities in the wrong place are unfounded.

Finally, let's apply the analogy of the canary in the coal mine. Before the invention of technical devices to detect odorless but deadly methane gas in deep mines, miners kept a caged canary nearby. As long as the bird was alive, gas was not present. However, if the bird died, it was a signal to the miners to get out immediately.

Likewise, we find that professional sports acts as a bellwether to our overall well-being. Highly paid athletes and the proliferation of professional teams are a signal that we are all better off. If those salaries begin to fall or large numbers of teams go bankrupt, however, beware: harder times are ahead for all.

> "*LeBron James had to feel that there was something going wrong in the Cavaliers front office in order for him to even consider leaving his home town.*"

Athletes Have a Right to Go for the Money and Success

Tangient LLC

In the following viewpoint, Tangient LLC argues in the defense of LeBron James to engage in The Decision, *a highly publicized and anticipated ESPN special in which the basketball star announced his intention to make the difficult choice of leaving the Cleveland Cavaliers to join the Miami Heat. Though James later stated his regret for the event, the author also lambasts team owner Dan Gilbert for his childish reaction. The author contends that it is the right of any human being to make career moves based on what is best for that person and that nobody has a right to criticize it simply in the name of loyalty.*

"The Decision," Tangient LLC. https://medialawandethicsfall11.wikispaces.com/ The+decision. Licensed under CC BY-SA 3.0.

As you read, consider the following questions:

1. How does the controversy surrounding the LeBron James *Decision* tie in with the subject matter of this chapter?
2. What arguments does the author use to defend James not only for leaving for Miami but for doing it in a highly publicized manner?
3. What terms does the author use to describe the motivations of James and Cavaliers owner Dan Gilbert throughout the free agency process and beyond?

The biggest free agency period/signing in NBA history took place last year but the results of this free agency is till this day under an enormous amount of criticism, and scrutiny. This legendary free agent class included professional basketball All-Stars such as Dwyane Wade, Dirk Nowitzki, Chris Bosh, Amar'e Stoudemire, Carlos Boozer and Joe Johnson. But the talk of the nation was about what two-time Most Valuable Player for the Cleveland Cavaliers; LeBron James was going to do with his first free agency. And the fact that he decided to make his decision into a one-hour special on ESPN, caused the criticism to flood the internet like Brazil going down in flames did to Twitter. But "The Decision" that LeBron James made is one of the most scrutinized and criticized things an NBA All Star has ever done in my lifetime.

A little bit over a year ago, on July 1st, 2010, to be exact, the NBA (Nation Basket Ball Association) annual free agency period started. In professional sports, a free agent is a player whose contract with a team has expired and who is thus eligible to sign with another club or franchise. At that time the current league MVP (Most Valuable Player), LeBron James was one of if not the most talked about free agent in what was already deemed the most legendary and historic free agent class of the NBA ever. "We've never had anything like this in my time that I can remember," New Jersey Nets president Rod Thorn said in an interview with ESPN. "There have been big-time free agents before, but never this many all at once, and at the same time this many teams that are trying to woo them. So it's unprecedented."

But what was even more unprecedented, and what some would call outrageous is just four days after the free agency period started, which was July 5th, LeBron James took to ESPN not to give his decision, but to announced that he planned to reveal the team with which he will sign during a one-hour special on ESPN, Thursday night, July 8th, 2010. Which would become a media phenomenon due to the fact that even though the basketball season was over, and the only Pro sport that are being played around that time is baseball, for an hour the whole world would have to sit and watch LeBron make his decision.

Right at that moment it seemed like the public opinion on LeBron changed instantly. King James had gone from being the most praised free agent, to being under mass amount of defamation within only one day. Defamation means to subject a person or group to public hatred, contempt and/or ridicule. LeBron was being defamed because the public, and media more importantly, where criticizing and slandering him by saying things that were not true about his character. Stating that he was only doing this "one-hour Decision special on ESPN," just for publicity, and for merely self pleasure, just to make a bigger name for himself. Which was false because James' publicist, Keith Estabrook, stated to *ESPN The Magazine*'s Chris Broussard that James himself requested he be allowed to sell sponsorship for the one-hour special, with the proceeds going to the Boys and Girls Clubs of America, and that ESPN agreed to the proposal.

Everyone and their mother started to point out LeBron's ego, his unfathomable self-concept bent out of control. The word "ridiculous" has been used about a zillion times along with other nastier words. James was construed as being overly self-important by the same people who have posted thousands of positive stories about him. But this was just the beginning of the defamation to LeBron James's character through both slander and libel.

Both the media and the public would yet turn up its criticism towards LeBron after his official decision. On July 8th, 2010, at 9 pm, in an hour long ESPN "Decision" special, after weeks of will-he-or-won't-he speculation, the two-time MVP stated "I've decided to take my talent down to South Beach," indicating he would join the Miami Heat and leave the Cavaliers after an unsuccessful seven-year quest for an NBA Championship ring.

Almost instantly, LeBron, (born of Akron Ohio, just 43 miles away from the city of Cleveland that drafted him No. 1 in 2003) went from home town King to public enemy number one.

Cleveland owner Dan Gilbert, in a letter to fans on the Cavs' website www.nba.com/cavaliers/, never mentions James by name, only referring to his nicknames in quotes and lambasting his former superstar for the way he announced his decision.

"This was announced with a several day, narcissistic, self-promotional build-up culminating with a national TV special of his 'decision' unlike anything ever 'witnessed' in the history of sports and probably the history of entertainment. Clearly, this is bitterly disappointing to all of us," Gilbert said in the letter.

"The good news is that the ownership team and the rest of the hard-working, loyal, and driven staff over here at your hometown Cavaliers have not betrayed you nor NEVER will betray you."

Gilbert, who has owned the Cavs for five years, said James' decision was a "cowardly betrayal" and called James the "self-titled former King'" and promised the No. 1 pick in the 2003 draft would be "taking the [Cleveland] 'curse' with him down south." "This shocking act of disloyalty from our home grown 'chosen one' sends the exact opposite lesson of what we would want our children to learn. And 'who' we would want them to grow up to become," Gilbert said.

"I PERSONALLY GUARANTEE THAT THE CLEVELAND CAVALIERS WILL WIN AN NBA CHAMPIONSHIP BEFORE THE SELF-TITLED FORMER 'KING' WINS ONE," Gilbert declared. "You can take it to the bank."

CONSIDER THE ATHLETE'S PERSPECTIVE

It appears that almost every day, a different NBA superstar is having his jersey tarnished by an angry group of disappointed and disgusted fans. LeBron James made the infamous "decision" in 2010 to join the Miami Heat, Kevin Durant completed his controversial move to the Golden State Warriors in 2016 and, most recently, Kyrie Irving demanded a trade out of Cleveland this past summer.

As devoted and passionate fans, it is easy to question the moral integrity of these players because we feel so emotionally invested in our favorite teams. But the fact of the matter is that the NBA is first and foremost a business. Although it is our first instinct to lash out with personal attacks on these players, we need to recognize as fans that it is impossible to understand the factors that prompt players to "betray" their teams.

Of course, owners can love the game of basketball, but the primary reason they invest their money into an organization is to earn a return on their investment. Players can display their loyalty and commitment to an organization as much as they want, but when it comes down to it, those in charge do not care what anyone's name is or what they've done for their team.

Basketball players are entertainers, and unlike musicians or actors who can work into their 70s, the window of opportunity for an NBA player is extremely limited. The average NBA career is only 4.8 years, according to Business Insider, so these professional players have limited time to make an impact.

Immediately after a player abandons his team, it is understandable that a die-hard fan would feel compelled to light his jersey on fire, or worse. But the next time a star departs for a new destination, take some time to consider the situation from the athlete's perspective.

"Column: Free Agency Decisions Spark Questions of Player Loyalty," by Marcus Budashewitz, Pipe Dream, November 16, 2017.

It is safe to say that Dan Gilbert feels the way LeBron went about his decision could be considered Consciousness Industry. Consciousness Industry is when the media is used to influence audiences to accept the policies of powerful people.

Now even though Dan Gilbert felt this was wrong on LeBron's part it is highly ethical. Because Professional Sports is just that, a profession, it's a business, The NBA is a company. LeBron James had to feel that there was something going wrong in the Cavaliers front office in order for him to even consider leaving his home town (where he was the star player, receiving the biggest contract of his career just to go to another star player's team and receive less money).

This is what LeBron had to say about why he chose to leave Cleveland for Miami. "I wanted to do what was best for me, what was best for LeBron James. At the end of the day, I feel awful. I feel even worse that I wasn't able to bring an NBA championship to that city. I never wanted to leave Cleveland. My heart will always be around that area. But I also felt like this is the greatest challenge for me. Winning is a huge thing for me, and I feel like Miami is the best place for me to win a Championship."

This is a fine example of Consequentialism, which is all about looking ahead. See LeBron feels like he did all he could do for the Cleveland Cavs, and in order to better his future he needed to leave [and] join the Miami Heat. This is also an example of Ethical Egoism which means doing what is best for yourself.

And the people of Cleveland were even more criticizing on LeBron's decision to leave. Their reaction was a sure sign of objectification. Objectification is the act of viewing or treating and individual as an item or commodity, as opposed to a human being. There were aria of Cleveland reactions to the LeBron decision including unhappiness, crying defamation of LeBron James character, riots and few even went as far as burning the number 23 LeBron James Cavs jerseys.

These fans clearly thought that LeBron should have stayed in Cleveland no matter what, because he was one of their own. They felt that this was his duty and obligation just as Immanuel Kant's theory of Enlightenment. This gives fine indication that the fans of Cleveland believe in Jeremy Bentham's theory of Utilitarianism. Utilitarianism means doing the greatest good for the greatest number of people. But the greatest good for the greater people wouldn't have been what John Stuart Mill indicates as quality of pleasure/happiness for the man ultimately making the decision, which was not the city of Cleveland nor the Cavs owner or its fans, but LeBron James.

I guess everyone would like LeBron to be more of an Ethical Altruist (Ethical Altruism means to never do for yourself, and to always seek to do what is best for others). But his Consequential "decision" to "Take my talents to South Beach" was in his best interest.

Periodical and Internet Sources Bibliography

The following articles have been selected to supplement the diverse views presented in this chapter.

Myles Brand, "Why the Fairness Argument on Pay for Play Isn't a Fair Argument," *Huffington Post*, May 25, 2011. https://www.huffingtonpost.com/myles-brand/why-the-fairness-argument_b_118386.html.

Kevin L. Burke, "Free Agent Fans: Do Allegiances Change When Favorite Players Leave?," Sporting News, December 8, 2016. http://www.sportingnews.com/other-sports/news/sports-fan-favorite-team-psychology-free-agents-players/ktcq8h2ae5rc1kr8f66ywo701.

CNN Wire, "The Athlete with the Biggest Contract May Surprise You," WGNO, March 31, 2017. https://wgno.com/2017/03/31/the-athlete-with-the-biggest-contract-may-surprise-you/.

Dom Cosentino, "Why Only the NFL Doesn't Guarantee Contracts," Deadspin, August 1, 2017. https://deadspin.com/why-only-the-nfl-doesnt-guarantee-contracts-1797020799.

Leland Faust, "Believe It or Not, Professional Athletes Are Actually Underpaid," *Sports Illustrated*, October 20, 2016. https://www.si.com/thecauldron/2016/10/20/professional-athletes-underpaid.

Steven Kutz, "In Pro Sports, Athletes in the 1% Are Getting Most of the Money Now Too," MarketWatch, March 17, 2017. https://www.marketwatch.com/story/in-pro-sports-athletes-in-the-1-are-getting-most-of-the-money-too-2017-03-17.

Alison Millington, "This Calculator Tells You How Long It Would Take the World's Highest-Paid Athletes to Earn Your Annual Salary—and for Most It's a Matter of Hours," Business Insider, January 11, 2018. http://www.businessinsider.com/calculator-shows-how-long-it-would-take-athletes-to-earn-your-salary-2018-1.

John Perritano, "How Does the NFL Salary Cap Work?," HuwStuffWorks, 2018. https://entertainment.howstuffworks.com/question6443.htm.

CHAPTER 3

What Responsibility Do Athletes Have to Their Leagues?

Chapter Preface

F airness. It is all fans ask of owners and players in the major American sports. Complaints abound about how the owners run the show and how the players often seek to give themselves a competitive edge.

After MLB players went on strike to protest salary caps in 1994, baseball had a financial and public relations problem. Team owners looked the other way when bulked-up sluggers used performance-enhancing drugs (PEDs) to rack up home runs in numbers never before conceived. The breaking of Roger Maris's single-season home run record resulted in the game returning to its good graces and fans flocking once again to ballparks. But those fans had been deceived. The allegations, often proven, that players such as Barry Bonds, Mark McGwire, Sammy Sosa, Roger Clemens, and Rafael Palmeiro had utilized PEDs to gain strength or rebound from injury had tossed away the most important bond any sports league has with its fans. And that is trust. It is no surprise that none of the players listed above—not even Bonds as the all-time career home run leader—has been voted into the Hall of Fame.

The issue of doping in baseball has since taken a back seat to competitive balance based on the lack of a salary cap. Yet one can argue in either direction on the effectiveness of such caps to create balance. It can be claimed with great validity that the NBA and NFL, both of which boast salary caps, are plagued with lower levels of competitive evenness than the MLB. The Golden State Warriors and Cleveland Cavaliers played in the NBA Finals three straight seasons from 2015 to 2017. Quarterback Tom Brady and his New England Patriots have been virtually annual participants in the Super Bowl. Yet twelve different teams have won the World Series since 2001.

Fairness in sports seems to be a moral issue, but its practicality often remains up for debate. Some fans even believe athletes should be allowed to take PEDs. They prefer to see their heroes maximize their potential and offer that it would even the playing field if everyone was given the green light. Most feel, however, that such immorality could ruin sports by creating a competitive imbalance. After all, PEDs are dangerous, and most athletes in this day and age better understand health concerns.

"*Of the ten World Series champions from 2001–2010, six ranked in the top ten in end of the year payroll. The remaining four teams all belonged to the middle ten.*"

Some Teams Have an Unfair Advantage

Northwestern Business Review

In the following viewpoint, Northwestern Business Review *uses in-depth statistics to explain why certain MLB teams can afford star players. The Yankees and Dodgers of the world spend hundreds of millions of dollars on free agents and on keeping their top home-grown talent for years, while the Royals and Rays of the world remain sidelined from the free agent bidding and must watch as their best players leave in free agency. The author contends that such an imbalance (both the Royals and Rays have been recent World Series participants, with the former having won a championship) in salaries has created a huge competitive imbalance.* Northwestern Business Review *is the leading business and tech publication of Northwestern University.*

"Why Certain MLB Teams Can Afford Star Players and Others Cannot," The Northwestern Business Review, January 3, 2012. Reprinted by permission.

As you read, consider the following questions:

1. Does this viewpoint give both sides of the issue of competitive balance in baseball?
2. What is the risk of creating a huge payroll for major league teams, according to this article?
3. Does the author offer any solutions to the perceived issue of competitive imbalance?

Major League Baseball's "Hot Stove" season is heating up. Former three time National League MVP Albert Pujols recently signed a ten-year contract with the Los Angeles Angels of Anaheim, worth over $250 million. Even some of the league's poorer teams have chosen to spend big this winter. The Miami Marlins committed nearly $200 million so far this off-season, signing shortstop and former National League batting champion Jose Reyes and pitchers Mark Buehrle and Heath Bell to free agent contracts. The Texas Rangers just paid $51.7 million just for the rights to negotiate with Japanese pitcher Yu Darvish. How can some teams, such as the Angels and the Rangers, afford to spend enormous amounts of money on star athletes, while others can only pay "scrubs" smaller salaries? And, more importantly, does the size of a team's payroll really matter?

Big and Small Market Teams: Why Are Some Team's Payrolls Larger than Others?

Sports writers and league employees typically refer to baseball teams as belonging to one of two groups: big-market teams and small-market teams. Specifically, the "big-market" designation refers to those teams that play in the nation's consolidated statistical metropolitan areas (CSMAs); "small-market" refers to teams that play in smaller CSMAs. In Major League Baseball, the New York Yankees, New York Mets, Chicago White Sox, Chicago Cubs, and the Boston Red Sox are undoubtedly "big-market" teams. The

Cincinnati Reds, Kansas City Royals, and Milwaukee Brewers are "small-market," teams while the rest fall somewhere in the middle.

While the size of the market refers only to the population of the respective city, it is also closely correlated, in most cases, to the amount of money that a team will spend on players. In general, teams in "big markets" attract more fans, allowing them to raise ticket prices. This is a simple principle of economics. The larger the fan base, the greater the demand for tickets. Ticket supply is relatively constant; a stadium can only hold so many people. As a result, prices rise. Larger ticket sales and higher ticket prices together increase a team's revenue, allowing team owners to reinvest more money into their organization while still turning a profit.

There are notable exceptions, however. Owners of big-market professional baseball teams may decide, for a number of reasons, to cut payroll and spend more like a middle-market or even small-market teams. For example, over the past few seasons, Fred Wilpon, the owner of the New York Mets, has lowered the team's payroll by many millions of dollars. On Opening Day of the 2009 MLB season, the Met's total payroll was over $135 million—the second highest in the league. At the start of the upcoming 2012 MLB season, the club's payroll is projected to be closer to $100 million.

On the other hand, small market teams sometimes overspend, hoping that a higher payroll—and the signing of marquee talent—will attract a larger fan base. For example, the Miami Marlins—previously the Florida Marlins—play in one of the league's smallest markets. (The team frequently struggles to draw fans and played a game in front of a dismal crowd of 347 this past August.) The Marlins, however, have rebranded themselves this year. The team will be moving to a new stadium for the 2012 season and recently released images of its new uniforms. Considering the circumstances, the Marlins' owner, Jeffery Loria, has spent a large amount of money so far this offseason; the 2012 Miami Marlins' payroll will be almost twice the team's 2011 payroll. The size of an organization's payroll is, in the end, completely up to its owner.

The Cost of Winning Games: Does a Larger Payroll Really Matter?

There is a clear gap between the league's richest teams and the league's poorer teams. At the beginning of the 2011 season, the New York Yankees had the league's highest payroll; an astonishing $202,689,028. Meanwhile, the league's poorest team—the Kansas City Royals—had a payroll of only $36,126,000. (To make the comparison even more shocking, consider this: the New York Yankees highest paid athlete last season was Alex Rodriguez who earned $32 million, almost as much as the entire Kansas City Royal's payroll.)

But does this payroll gap really matter? Recently, CNBC's sports business journalist (and Northwestern alum) Darren Rovell reported a study focusing on this very issue. During the period from 2001–2010, 61.5% of the league's playoff teams were among the top 10 biggest spenders; 23.1% ranked 11th–20th in total end of the year payroll and 15.4% were among the league's poorest 10 teams. The evidence is clear: teams in the top third in overall payroll have almost twice the chance of reaching the playoffs than other teams.

The data is even more startling when examining the payrolls of World Series winners. Of the ten World Series champions from 2001–2010, six ranked in the top ten in end of the year payroll. The remaining four teams all belonged to the middle ten.

While a team doesn't have to be the league's richest to win the World Series—the New York Yankees had the highest payroll each year from 2001–2010 and won only one World Series (2009)—teams generally benefit from having a higher payroll.

Despite the general trend, there have been examples that defy the common logic. Rich teams have crashed and burned; the New York Mets, for example, have accumulated a payroll of over $100 million each of the last few seasons, but have not made the playoffs since 2006. Last year, with a payroll of nearly $119 million, the Mets won only seventy-seven games, and by the end of the season was barely competitive. Less commonly, poor teams have succeeded, playing over their heads and exceeding expectations. By example, in the early 2000s, the Oakland Athletics, with one of the lowest payrolls in the game, ranked at or near the top of Major League Baseball in total wins.

Creating Competitive Balance: Major League Baseball's Collective Bargaining Agreement

Major League Baseball's collective bargaining agreement (CBA) includes multiple conditions that, when read together, attempt to create competitive balance. First, the league's collective bargaining agreement puts in place a system of revenue sharing. Under the system, the league redistributes wealth away from richer teams towards poorer teams. Every team is required to deposit a percentage of their local revenues into a pot at the end of each season. Luxury tax funds and a portion of the league's "Central Fund"—comprised of monies from television contracts and the like—are also put into the pot. The pot is then redistributed amongst the thirty different teams, with poorer teams—such as the Oakland Athletics and Pittsburgh Pirates—receiving larger portions of the pot.

While the league's revenue sharing system succeeds in redistributing wealth, it does not significantly improve parity amongst the teams. Rich teams still spend large amounts of money on team payroll, regardless of revenue sharing. While it can be argued that revenue sharing is meant to benefit poorer teams rather than penalize richer teams, the system fails. In many cases, teams receiving large portions of the pot misuse the funds. Rather than investing in a higher payroll and signing better talent, MLB organizations sometimes use the shared revenue to otherwise increase profits.

More importantly, the league's CBA implements a luxury tax. Simply put, organizations that spend over a specified amount of money in total payroll face a monetary penalty for their actions. The luxury tax threshold varies from year to year and is stipulated in the CBA. For the upcoming 2012 season, the threshold is $178 million. The amount paid depends on the offense. First time offenders must pay 22.5% of salaries above the threshold. Second times offenders must pay 30% and third (and sequent) time offenders must pay 40% of salaries above the threshold.

While the luxury tax attempts to deter teams from spending huge amounts of money, it has had little effect in increasing parity between big- and small-market teams. Since the tax was first implemented in 2003, only four organizations have been penalized. Over the nine-year period, the New York Yankees have paid over $192 million in penalties. The Boston Red Sox have been penalized approximately $15 million, the Los Angeles Angels of Anaheim $1.3 million, and the Detroit Tigers under $1 million.

Why has the luxury tax proven ineffective? The most likely answer is that the threshold has been placed too high. The average team payroll at the beginning of the 2011 season was approximately $93 million, just over half of the luxury tax threshold. Moreover, only three teams were even close to the limit: the New York Yankees ($202.7 million), the Philadelphia Phillies ($173 million), and the Boston Red Sox ($161.8 million).

Improving the System: What Does Major League Baseball Need to Do to Achieve Competitive Balance?

Major League Baseball's current luxury tax has done little to improve the league's competitive balance, but would the league benefit from a different, more stringent system? Should Major League Baseball adopt a salary cap? Of the nations four major professional sports leagues, MLB is the only league without a true salary cap. The NHL adopted a hard salary cap for the 2005–06 season. Under the new CBA adopted in the summer of 2011, the NFL also adopted a hard salary cap of $120 million and a salary floor of $108 million. The NBA's salary cap is a "soft" cap;

teams cannot spend above a certain payroll threshold except in the case of certain "exceptions," included in the league's new collective bargaining agreement. For example, under the "Larry Bird" rule, teams are allowed to spend above the maximum payroll in order to re-sign their own free agents.

While evidence on competitive balance in the NHL, NFL, and NBA is scarce—the NFL and NBA are in the first year of their new CBAs—the systems draw an interesting comparison to MLB's luxury tax. A hard salary cap is an interesting option, disallowing teams from spending above a predetermined amount under any circumstances. However, if MLB were to adopt a hard salary cap with a threshold similar to the current luxury tax threshold—as one might assume—the cap would be ineffective, restricting the spending of only a few teams. Similarly, a soft cap would also prove ineffective. In essence, MLB's luxury tax is a form of a soft cap. Teams are given a threshold that they are not allowed to exceed. If teams choose to generate a payroll above the threshold, they are penalized or taxed. The tax is like the exceptions present in the NBA's soft cap.

The system currently in place under the NFL's CBA provides the best solution the Major League Baseball's concerns. Not only will teams be disallowed from generating a high payroll, but they would also be banned from spending too little money on major league talent. The system could be particularly effective in MLB, where astonishingly low payrolls are almost as big of a problem as high payrolls.

Unfortunately, Major League Baseball seems particularly hesitant towards adopting a hard salary cap or a salary floor of any kind. In the recent labor talks that concluded in early December, team owners and the league's players' association debated the institution of a luxury tax in reverse. Under the proposed system, there would be a threshold at the lower end of the payroll scale. Teams that spend below the threshold would be hit with a tax, just as teams that spend above the current luxury tax threshold are penalized. Not surprisingly, the system was not adopted. Team owners—particularly the owners of the league's poorer teams—want the ability and opportunity to keep costs down.

With a new CBA adopted only a month ago, Major League Baseball's luxury tax system will remain in place for at least the next five seasons, effectively ensuring that a competitive balance will not be achieved.

> "A hard salary cap and lower ticket
> prices ... would mean players would
> have to sacrifice some earnings either
> now or in the future, [but] it would
> prevent a cap from transferring
> revenue from players to owners."

The MLB Needs a Salary Cap

Duncan Weinstein

In the following viewpoint, Duncan Weinstein argues for a cap to rein in soaring player salaries. The author argues that, although the MLB is still profitable, the sport of baseball is waning in importance in American culture. He suggests that, to make attendance more affordable and accessible to the public, the league should pursue greater competitive balance. Among the complaints about the sport is that many in the lower economic strata of society cannot afford to attend games. The problem is particularly acute in the African American community, which might explain poor attendance among blacks and the distinct lack of African American players in the sport as compared to the 1970s. Weinstein is a graduate of Brown University.

"Weinstein '17: Why MLB Needs a Hard Salary Cap," by Duncan Weinstein, Brown Daily Herald, March 31, 2015. Reprinted by permission.

As you read, consider the following questions:

1. How does the author go beyond the realm of competitive balance when arguing for a hard salary cap in major league baseball?
2. Does the viewpoint explain why the major league players' union has consistently rejected any salary cap during contract negotiations?
3. How much did team payrolls increase from 1998 to 2014, according to the viewpoint?

O pening Day is next week, but it's unlikely anyone will be taking me out to the ball game this year. That's because average ticket prices have increased from $14.94 in 1998—when a player signed a $100 million contract for the first time—to $27.93 in 2014, adjusted to 2014 dollars. While prices vary greatly throughout the season and between teams, the fact is it's more expensive to see a live game than it used to be. A family trip to the ballpark can easily run above $100, making major league baseball inaccessible even as a special treat for many families.

Since the 1994 players strike, player salaries and payrolls have increased dramatically. Pitcher Kevin Brown became the first player to sign a nine-figure contract, inking a seven-year, $100 million deal with the Dodgers in 1998. Two years later, Alex Rodriguez signed a 10-year, $252 million contract with the Texas Rangers, making him baseball's highest paid player until the Miami Marlins committed $325 million to outfielder Giancarlo Stanton over 13 years last November. The league's average salary has nearly doubled from $2 million in 1998 to $3.8 million last year, adjusted to 2014 dollars, according to ESPN.

As salaries have increased, so too have payrolls. In 1998, the average opening day payroll was $59.5 million in 1998 compared to $115 million in 2014, in 2014 dollars. According to a study by the Harvard Sports Analysis Collective, the Gini coefficient—a tool economists use to measure inequality—of MLB team payrolls has increased since the mid-1990s. Payroll isn't destiny, but it makes a big difference. Teams like the Rays and Athletics can't afford the big-ticket free agents commonly found in Yankee or Dodger uniforms.

Some, like Ben McGrath in the *New Yorker* and Jonathan Mahler in the *New York Times*, have commented on baseball's declining importance in American culture, even if the league remains profitable for now. Some see the slow pace of the game as dooming it to irrelevance in the 21st century. More than any other American sport, baseball is self-consciously nostalgic and traditional. You have to grow up with baseball to understand and appreciate it.

In high school, I took my then-girlfriend, an Argentine, to a Chicago Cubs game at Wrigley Field. I loved every minute of it, and she asked to leave in the sixth inning. People watch baseball not just for pitch-and-catch but also for the strategy, the atmosphere and the tradition. The key to keeping baseball relevant is to keep it present in peoples' lives. A big part of that comes down to ticket prices.

Of course, compared to 2014 average ticket prices of $84.43 for the NFL, $62.18 for the NHL and $53.98 for the NBA, according to league data from statistics company Statista, baseball is much more affordable. But what matters is not just relative affordability but objective affordability.

If baseball is to thrive economically and culturally, it needs to reach a new generation of fans and potential players. Taking kids to professional games is one way of doing that, since baseball fandom is especially dependent on watching live games. Already, the MLB is suffering from the disappearance of one kind of diversity: The percentage of African-American players has declined from about 18 percent in the 1970s and '80s to less than half that figure today.

Baseball would benefit if the owners agreed to a hard salary cap and lower ticket prices. While this would mean players would have to sacrifice some earnings either now or in the future, it would prevent a cap from transferring revenue from players to owners. MLB players are already some of the world's highest paid athletes, making much more money with much less injury risk than football players.

An agreement could work something like this: A cap in the $150–220 million range, with steadily lower ticket prices as television revenues continue to increase. It's important the cap stay high for now, to avoid penalizing teams that have already committed a lot of money to players. But when Giancarlo Stanton's contract, the longest in baseball, expires in 13 years, the league could move the cap even lower, or just let inflation eat at a solid cap. That way, a greater diversity of fans can enjoy the game and even have a little money left over for peanuts and cracker jacks.

> "*The government allows American sports leagues to maintain a national monopoly in a way allowed in almost no other industry, and it accepts policies like salary caps that would normally run afoul of antitrust laws.*"

Team Owners Are Reaping Most of the Rewards

Jim Pagels

In the following viewpoint, Jim Pagels provides a more in-depth study of salary caps in sports as compared to rules and laws that restrict other American industries. This unbiased account gives an explanation as to why sports leagues can regulate team salaries while other businesses cannot. Pagels explains that the basis of sports is competition, thereby altering the playing field. He gives both sides of the argument for and against the salary cap in the NFL and NBA, as well as the lack of one in the MLB. He therefore allows the readers to decide for themselves on the viability of the salary cap in various leagues. Pagels is an economics researcher who writes about economics and sports.

"Are Salary Caps for Professional Athletes Fair?" by Jim Pagels, Priceonomics.com, August 19, 2014. Reprinted by permission.

As you read, consider the following questions:

1. What is the strongest argument cited by the author in legitimizing the salary cap in professional sports?
2. What is the strongest argument cited by the author against the use of a salary cap in professional sports?
3. How does the author explain why competition allows sports leagues to utilize salary caps while other businesses cannot?

A ntitrust laws exist to prevent businesses from conspiring to artificially limit demand, set prices, or restrict pay. Earlier this year, a US District Court forced Apple, Google, Intel and Adobe to pay $325 million in a class action lawsuit for agreeing not to poach each other's employees. There is one industry, though, where wide-scale collusion is not only legal, but universal: professional sports. Salary caps, which exist in most leagues, are one of several mechanisms that allow a club of billionaire sports team owners to collectively control and suppress the wages of millionaire young athletes. How did this come about, and are they effective? Could leagues function without them? And under what pretenses can billionaire owners argue that they need to collectively suppress wages?

The key difference between sports and other industries is that competition is the product that leagues sell. If teams could purchase victories or if the Vegas odds always favored the same teams, then the value of that competition would decline. In other words, New York Yankees tickets would not be nearly as valuable if they played against Little League teams. (Although the first game would be entertaining.)

For this reason, leagues argue that they must sustain some degree of parity between their teams, and they claim to accomplish this through revenue sharing, entry-level player drafts, and, most of all, salary caps—limits on the amount of money teams can spend on players.

The History of Salary Caps

Salary caps are a relatively new phenomenon. Before the introduction of free agency in the 1980s, many leagues, most notably Major League Baseball, operated under the "reserve clause," which prohibited players from negotiating with other teams, even after the conclusion of a contract. Players challenged this clause in the 1970s, and owners offered many of the same arguments then that they do today about salary caps:

> "... owners of sports teams developed the argument that, whatever the consequences of the reserve clause on players' salaries, it was needed to preserve competitive balance. Owners argued that free agency would allow the richest teams to acquire a disproportionate share of the playing talent in the league. Competitive balance would be destroyed, driving weaker franchises out of business."

By the 1980s, free agency was in vogue, and with this, owners soon introduced a more modern labor control too: salary caps. Today, the NFL and NHL both have hard caps, which means that no team can exceed a certain spending limit. Under the NBA's soft cap, teams can exceed the cap, but only to retain their own players—a clause known as the "Larry Bird Exception" as the Boston Celtics used this rule to retain Bird for his entire career. The MLB only has a (very forgiving) luxury tax—a threshold above which teams must pay a certain percentage in penalty for every dollar they spend over the limit. In the 11-year history of the tax, only five teams have ever paid, with the Yankees' payments constituting 95% of that total.

As sports have become more lucrative, salary caps have increased. Today, salary caps are controversial. Its critics often argue on the grounds of antitrust, but the existence depends on whether you view a league's franchises as a single, unified entity or a collection of individual firms. This classification came up in the 1922 *Baltimore Federal Baseball Club v. National League* case, in which a unanimous ruling held baseball exempt from antitrust laws. Nearly a century later, the courts delivered a different decision in the 2010 *American Needle v. NFL* Supreme Court case, which declared that the NFL's collective apparel licensing was in fact subject to examination under the Sherman Antitrust Act.

The Case for Salary Caps

Salary cap proponents argue that caps are effective and necessary. They give poorer, small-market teams a chance to compete, and this competitive balance draws in fans and benefits the league as a whole.

A substantial body of academic literature supports this claim. A 2011 paper in *Economic Inquiry* that investigated salary caps, salary floors, and revenue sharing found that "the effect on club profits, player salaries, and competitive balance crucially depends on the mix of these policy tools." Another 2011 University of Alabama paper that focused on baseball argued that the sport has a severe competitive balance issue that negatively affects fan interest. Other studies have shown that salary caps have effectively promoted competitive balance and concluded that forbidding leagues from operating as a single entity would hurt revenues.

The case for salary caps is strongest for sports in which the correlation between money and wins is relatively strong. There have been countless analytic studies on this subject, and they have largely shown that these strong relationships occur in sports with a) small year-to-year variation in player performance, which makes it easier to accurately spend money and b) a large season sample size so that inferior (often poorer) teams are weeded out.

[Taking] an example of the money vs. performance relationship in the NFL (a league with narrow talent variation, a 16-game season, and single game playoffs) and the NBA (a league with wide talent variation, an 82-game season, and 7-game playoff series):

As expected, the NFL—which still has variation in spending despite a hard cap—has a rather weak money vs. performance correlation compared to the NBA. (The correlation in the NBA would be much stronger if not for a maximum salary on individual players, which artificially limits their value and allows General Managers to assemble super-teams under the cap.) The stronger NBA correlation suggests that in the absence of spending restrictions, teams might gain a significant edge, which could cause overall league revenues—and in turn player salaries—to decline as a select few teams in large markets or with wealthy owners dominate each and every year.

There's historical precedent for this concern: In 1884, the Union Associated baseball league folded after a single season when the St. Louis Maroons ran away with first place by 21 games. Similarly, theAll-America Football Conference folded after four years in the late 1940s. The Cleveland Browns tore through the league, losing only three games in four years—a performance so dominant that it literally destroyed the league.

Cap proponents also point to modern examples like the English Premier League (EPL), where a lack of spending restrictions has led to incredible disparity between payrolls. The wealthiest clubs buy up the best players and dominate; only four teams (Manchester United, Manchester City, Chelsea, and Arsenal) have won the league since 1995. (Those four teams also largely dominate the 2nd- and 3rd-place finishes.)

With this extreme inequality, the EPL reportedly took in over $5 billion in revenue last year—half that of the NFL—with much of that revenue concentrated among the top 4–5 teams while mid- and smaller-tier clubs languished. However, the Union of European Football Associations recently announced a set of regulations known as Financial Fair Play to balance spending among the top teams. Deloitte describes the new protocols effect in the 23rd edition of the *Annual Review of Football Finance*:

> The signs are that most clubs are adopting a more financially robust and balanced approach to the way they run their businesses, and they must continue down this path if they are to safeguard the long-term financial health of the game.

Along these lines, cap proponents often argue that financial restraint is necessary to keep franchises—and their valuable brand identities—afloat for generations. In largely restriction-free English soccer, there is a vast graveyard of defunct clubs, many of which spent themselves into oblivion. The sink-or-swim spending atmosphere of the Football League Championship—the second-tier league below the EPL— has led nine of its 24 teams to employ player payrolls greater than that of their revenues, endangering long-term stability. Comparatively, in the four major American sports, no team has folded since the Dallas Texans closed shop back in 1952.

Cap proponents also claim that parity is necessary to grow fan bases across the country, and the numbers back this up. A 2009 article in the *Journal of Sports Economics* noted that "winning is an important determinant of attendance" for all 12 MLB teams in the study, and randomness and unexpected outcomes—common in leagues with great parity—attract eyeballs. While those opposed to caps argue that fans watch any game with the slightest uncertainty in its outcome, this ignores the larger picture. Yes, any individual game will always have some uncertainty, but postseason races or playoff series can easily be all but decided, and the data suggests that this inevitability turns away fans.

NBA playoff game TV ratings spike when the series is close, but they are far lower when one team takes a near-decisive lead. [In an example taking] the average TV rating by leverage, a metric that measures the importance of a playoff game in swinging a series, for all 250 playoff games from 2011-2013: Running a regression on this data, controlling for year, time, market size, round, and TV channel, shows game number in the series and leverage—both indicators of a close matchup—to be highly indicative of ratings. Similarly, MLB teams that fall out of contention early see their attendance languish in the second half of the season. Sure, the battle may be always in doubt, but if the war is all but decided, viewers appear to tune out.

The Case Against Salary Caps

Those against salary caps argue that a group of firms shouldn't have the power to collude against labor wages and that salary caps do not enforce league parity, but instead merely tamp down costs for wealthy teams. In other words, caps are discounts for billionaires.

It's not too difficult to see the logic behind this. In a completely free market, high-revenue teams would bid each other up to high figures for elite players, but salary caps serve as an insurance policy against each other. In uncapped baseball, Miguel Cabrera, worth only 5–7 extra wins per season (out of 162), can sign a 10-year, $292 million contract. Meanwhile, LeBron James's value to his team is many multiples of Cabrera.

However, for the majority of his prime, LeBron has made roughly half what Cabrera now earns, and the four-time NBA MVP has taken notice. (It's worth noting that the average NBA salary is actually far greater than that of MLB, but much of this is simply due to splitting revenue between far fewer players in basketball. Also, this extreme devaluation of NBA star talent is in some extent due to the overall league salary cap, but more so due to the individual maximum player salary, an extremely constricting clause that dramatically decreases parity as it facilitates the creation of super teams by allowing them to fit multiple salary-controlled superstars under the cap—something teams could never do without such measures. LeBron isn't teaming up with Dwyane Wade and Chris Bosh if he can go make $45 million a year playing in Phoenix or Denver.)

Salary cap opponents also argue that spending restrictions are ineffective—if not outright detrimental—at achieving their intended goal of parity. David Berri, author of *The Wages of Wins*, finds that the implementation of caps and luxury taxes in the NBA, NFL, NHL, and MLB had a statistically insignificant impact on parity. He also calculates that perfect balance in the MLB would only result in a 15% increase in attendance. Similarly, a 2011 paper in the *Journal for Economic Educators* found that a cap in the NBA would actually hurt competitive balance, most likely due to exemptions which restrict player movement, and showed that revenue sharing is a much more effective way to institute parity. (The effects of revenue sharing on profit maximization and parity enforcement has been highly debated.)

At the furthest extreme, one study by antitrust economist Andy Schwartz noted that with all monetary incentives perfectly equal (at zero), college football severely obstructs the Coase theorem, which states that labor will find its way to locations in which it has the greatest utility, and has inequality on par with that found in the EPL. Other critics contend that salary caps and revenue sharing coddle underperforming franchises. Since owners know that losing seasons won't put them out of business, these policies reduce the incentive to win. Rather than the EPL's "sink-or-swim" format, American sports have more of a "swim-or-repeatedly tread water" approach.

Those against caps also note that playoffs encourage competitive balance in terms of championship totals. Elimination games or series spur randomness and frequently allow inferior (often low-revenue) teams to prevail in small sample sizes.

The need for spending limits will vary by sport, but the strongest case against a cap comes in the only game without one: baseball. Due to the sport's inherent randomness—even over the course of a 162-game season—it's extremely difficult to accurately spend money on player talent. In 2013, the correlation between player salary and performance was nearly zero.

While the concept of winning an "unfair game" was popularized by Michael Lewis's 2003 book, *Moneyball*, lack of large payroll certainly hasn't been too big a detriment for many teams. In fact, recent articles in *The Hardball Times* and *Freakonomics* show that the relationship between money and wins has decreased over time.

Are Caps Fair?

In negotiating salary caps, most leagues split mandatory sport-specific revenue roughly 50–50 between owners and players. In recent years, players have agreed to accept a smaller slice of the pie. In both the most recent NBA and NHL labor negotiations, players went from receiving 57% of basketball- and hockey-related income to 50% while NFL players went from a 50/50 split to 47%. When factoring in total league revenues, players' shares are slightly smaller, but roughly equal across sports.

If caps or luxury taxes were removed, would players earn more? A 2007 *Southern Economic Journal* study found that revenue redistribution lowered MLB salaries by roughly 22% and had little effect on parity. In the NBA, the effect is likely stronger as over a dozen teams regularly brush up against an extremely punitive luxury tax and jockey for strategic revenue-sharing positions lower on the payroll rankings.

A 50/50 split may seem fair at first glance, but a number of arguments make the case that owners receive far too much of the pie.

The players' declining share of revenue resulted from owners playing hardball in recent lockouts, as players realized that holding out for a higher share of revenues was not worth missing part of the season. After all, any additional revenue players could earn in the future would be negated by lost wages in the present. This provided owners with a huge bargaining advantage. While the players have limited career windows to earn money in the league, the owners have their entire lives and can afford to use this time advantage as leverage.

Owners also have the advantage of being the only show in town, as no viable alternative leagues exist to draw players. Leagues with competition have not had as much success implementing caps. The English Premiership rugby league installed a cap in 1999, but many of its star players moved to Japan and France, where spending was not restricted.

Back to LeBron for a moment: The NBA superstar, who currently makes $20.6 million per year in the NBA, famously expressed interest in playing in Europe should someone offer a $50 million annual salary. The idea was not outlandish. James's salary is limited by restrictions on maximum player salaries, there are some very wealthy European owners, and his true financial worth is estimated at between $40 and $50 million, even under the cap. No deal materialized, so James continues to play in the United States.

(Staying in America, however, would probably always be LeBron's best option. While the four-time MVP has made only $126 million in salary over his career, he has also made $326 million in endorsements by playing in the most famous basketball league on the planet. It would be difficult to match that figure while playing in a little-known European league. One could argue that these endorsement opportunities are so profitable due to relative parity, which drives the NBA's universal popularity.)

Owners always bring up annual revenues and costs when negotiating a salary cap, but only focusing on those figures is extremely shortsighted. When you consider that teams in every sport are rapidly gaining value, franchises could actually lose quite a bit of money each year, and owners would still make large capital gains to recoup those losses.

One could also ask whether sports franchises should turn a profit at all, given their status as luxury toys for billionaires. Owning a professional sports team is not like owning an insurance company; it's more like owning a rare painting or a Ferrari—a status symbol. If the NBA approached a group of wealthy businessmen and said, "Ignore profits and just focus on this: You'll become an instant celebrity, sit courtside at every game, and hang out with superstar athletes. How much would you pay for that lifestyle?" that would surely fetch a high price.

Malcolm Gladwell discusses this subject in a 2011 Grantland story, in which he notes that economists call these extra perks of owning something like a sports team "psychic benefits":

> *Forbes* magazine annually estimates the value of every professional franchise, based on standard financial metrics like operating expenses, ticket sales, revenue, and physical assets like stadiums. When sports teams change hands, however, the actual sales price is invariably higher. *Forbes* valued the Detroit Pistons

at $360 million. They just sold for $420 million. *Forbes* valued the Wizards at $322 million. They just sold for $551 million. *Forbes* said that the Warriors were worth $363 million. They just sold for $450 million. There are a number of reasons why the *Forbes* number is consistently too low. The simplest is that *Forbes* is evaluating franchises strictly as businesses. But they are being bought by people who care passionately about sports—and the $90 million premium that the Warriors' new owners were willing to pay represents the psychic benefit of owning a sports team.

With these these points in mind, you can make a strong case that teams should not only lose money each year, but actually lose quite a bit of money. So while salary caps are hotly contested, we can offer some answers to the questions that motivated this article.

Are salary caps necessary? It depends on the sport, with randomness and season length being primary factors. In baseball, where greater financial resources is no guarantee of success, the MLB has done fine in terms of parity with limited restrictions. If the NBA got rid of all spending controls, however, deep-pocketed teams in New York and L.A. would inevitably dominate.

Are salary caps fair? Almost never—at least at current levels. The government allows American sports leagues to maintain a national monopoly in a way allowed in almost no other industry, and it accepts policies like salary caps that would normally run afoul of antitrust laws. Part of the onus on fighting this status quo lies on players' unions to bring up psychic benefits at the CBA negotiating table. Another may involve wealthy investors starting their own leagues with more favorable player salaries—or perhaps, as one paper suggests, the government forcibly splitting up leagues as it once split up oil, aluminum, and tobacco cartels.

Having said that, the evidence suggests that some form of spending restrictions or revenue sharing is probably best for the quality and financial interests of the game. Sports owners, however, have arguably abused that leniency by extracting far too high a share of league revenues, even as there's a line around the block of wealthy investors ready to throw down vast sums for sports franchises the moment they come up for sale to acquire the immense capital gains, annual profits, and perhaps most importantly, status and lifestyle that come with them.

That's one more telling detail about the current state of affairs: Hundreds of players come and go every year, but owners cling on to franchises for life and routinely pass them down to their children after death. While there have been high-profile sales of the Los Angeles Clippers, Buffalo Bills, and Milwaukee Bucks in recent years, it's rare teams actually hit the open market. Owners know how great a deal they're getting—they get to own a fun toy that also appreciates in value. That's not something they're going to part with anytime soon.

> "Owners are still demanding
> salary concessions in the name of
> competitive balance. And as noted
> in the past, owners of professional
> sports teams have made this
> argument since the 1870s."

Do NBA Owners Care About Balance?

Dave Berri

In the following viewpoint, Dave Berri maintains that only greed and not their stated drive for competitive balance motivates NBA owners to maintain a salary cap. Among the statistics and other facts he cites is that teams in the smaller markets have succeeded on the court with as high a level of consistency as their big-market brethren, though one might counter that that is the result of a salary cap, not despite it. The struggles in recent seasons of huge-market clubs such as the New York Knicks and the Los Angeles Lakers certainly add fuel to both sides of the argument. Berri is an economics professor at Southern Utah University and was president of the North American Association of Sports Economists.

"NBA Owners Do Not Understand Competitive Balance," by Dave, The Wages of Wins Journal, August 10, 2011. Reprinted by permission.

As you read, consider the following questions:

1. How effectively does the author argue against the salary cap in the NBA?
2. Does the author make a strong claim that NBA owners care little about competitive balance?
3. How does the author use comparisons to the MLB, NFL, and NHL to strengthen his case?

I n the July 25th edition of *Sports Illustrated* we saw the following statement (from a story about Derek Fisher and the NBA labor dispute):

> The league contends that owners and players together will grow financially and thrive in competitive balance as long as the richest teams aren't permitted to overspend and the smallest markets are assured of profitability.

This one sentence seems to suggest much that is inconsistent with the evidence. To see this, here is what I think we know about competitive balance in the NBA.

1. The NBA—Relative to the Other Major North American Sports—Is Relatively Imbalanced. And This Has Been True Throughout the Tenure of David Stern.

Roger Noll and Gerald Scully developed a measure of competitive balance that involves calculating the ratio between the level of competitive balance we observe and the ideal level of balance (the calculation is detailed in many places, including *The Wages of Wins*). For the NBA, here is the average value for this ratio in the 27 years since Stern became commissioner (in 1984) and the 27 years before Stern took over the NBA (Editor's Note: In a perfect world the measure would be 1.0).

- Competitive balance ratio in the NBA from 1984–85 to 2010–11: 2.8

- Competitive balance ratio in the NBA from 1957–58 to 1983–84: 2.5

So the NBA, both before and after Stern, has consistently had a ratio in excess of 2.0. To put that in perspective, here is the same snap-shot for the NHL, NFL, and both leagues in baseball.

- NHL: 1.7 since 1984, 2.1 before 1984
- NFL: 1.5 both before and after 1984
- AL: 1.8 both before and after 1987
- NL: 1.7 since 1984 and 1.8 before 1984

As one can see, the other sports have generally had a ratio below 2.0. And that means—relative to other North American sports—the NBA is not very balanced.

One should note that historically baseball used to look like the NBA today. In the first half of the 20th century, the AL and NL both had an average ratio of around 2.4. How baseball improved—and how the NBA has not—is important to our explanation of what drives competitive balance. Before we get to that story, though, let's talk about what doesn't seem to drive balance in a sports league.

2. Salary Caps, Payroll Caps, Luxury Taxes, and Revenue Sharing Don't Seem to Have Much Impact on Competitive Balance.

David Stern and the NBA owners want to impose further limits on the spending of owners in the NBA. The NBA (in 1984) was the first to impose any kind of cap on team payroll. And in 1999 the NBA was the first leage to cap the salaries of individual players. As one can see, the 1984 cap didn't alter competitive balance. And since 1999, the average ratio in the NBA has been 2.7. So the 1999 salary cap also didn't seem to have much impact on balance.

This is not a surprising result. Martin Schmidt and I presented research this past summer that looked at the impact of various institutions (i.e. salary caps, luxury taxes, etc. …) the NBA, NHL, NFL, and Major League Baseball have created to alter competitive balance. We found that none of these institutions had any statistically significant impact on balance in any of these leagues.

One should add that Martin and I are not the only researchers to look at how league institutions impact balance. Tony Krautmann and John Solow published research recently that indicated that increased revenue sharing in baseball also failed to impact competitive balance. Krautmann and Solow, though, did find that revenue sharing reduces the wages paid to players.

So the institutions that leagues use reduce wages but don't seem to change competitive balance. Before moving on, let's briefly note what seems to drive balance in a league. As we have shown in past research (and as discussed in *The Wages of Wins*), competitive balance in a league [is] primarily about changes in the population leagues draw upon for talent. For example, racial integration had a positive impact on competitive balance in baseball. And an influx of foreign talent in hockey (as Marty and I noted in our research this summer) led to more balance in the NHL.

Although the NBA also draws upon foreign talent, the impact on balance isn't seen because the population basketball teams draw upon—even when we consider the entire world—is still quite small. Specifically, NBA teams require really tall athletes. And since tall athletes are in short supply, the NBA persistently has a problem with balance. In other words, the supply of dominant players—like LeBron James and Dwight Howard—is quite small. Some teams get these amazing players. And others have to employ players like Andrea Bargnani and Travis Outlaw.

3. There Is No Relationship Between Market Size and Team Wins.

The NBA has one team located in Salt Lake City (1.1 million people in metropolitan area) and one team located in Chicago (9.6 million people in metropolitan area). Such disparities in market size lead people to suspect that teams located in smaller markets are at a competitive disadvantage. But when we look at the average number of wins from 1999–00 to 2010–11 and the population in each metropolitan area, we fail to find a statistically significant link. In sum, market size and on-court success are not related.

One can also look at payroll and wins across this same time period. We do find a statistically significant link between team spending and wins. But team payroll only explains 6% of the variation in team wins. In other words, teams are not able to effectively buy wins in the NBA.

4. Fans Don't Seem to Care Much About Competitive Balance.

But what if the richest teams could actually buy wins effectively? Wouldn't that cause a problem for the league?

Researchers have looked at the link between competitive balance and league attendance in baseball. As noted in *The Wages of Wins*, the link is quite small. Two different studies found that in baseball, a movement from the most competitive position in league history to the least competitive position in league history would only result in about a 15% increase in attendance. Yes, that is something. But that is all you get from a move from the least balanced position to the most balance.

Recently I have looked at this same issue in the NBA. And the preliminary results seem quite similar. NBA fans don't seem to care much about competitive balance. To illustrate, the NBA was much more balanced in the late 1970s, but it was not very popular. As noted, since Stern took over the NBA has not been balanced at all. And yet per game attendance has risen from about 11,000 in 1983–84 to more than 17,000 this past season. Furthermore, the league's television contract has risen from less than $40 million per year (for the entire league) in 1984 to more than $900 million per year today.

Despite all this evidence, though, owners are still demanding salary concessions in the name of competitive balance. And as noted in the past, owners of professional sports teams have made this argument since the 1870s. So it is not surprising to see this story being told. But one hopes is understood—at least someday—is that the owner's argument is not supported by the empirical evidence.

Let me close with an unrelated note from the aforementioned *Sports Illustrated* article. The following paragraph from the article clearly has a *Wages of Wins* theme:

> The owners maintain that a hard ceiling on team salaries is crucial, citing the failure of even the luxury tax to curb teams' overspending. Fisher says that a hard cap would encourage each team to budget the majority of its payroll for two or three stars, leaving other players to not only compete for the remaining money but also to do so largely on nonguaranteed contracts. "What we envision is a cannibalist-type system, where you would constantly be in competition with your teammates over shots and points and minutes," says Fisher. "We've had a problem over the years convincing fans that guys really do care about playing as a team and wanting to make a sacrifice to win a championship and not just thinking about themselves."

The Wages of Wins argued that salary in the NBA was primarily driven by scoring. And this argument was echoed in *Stumbling on Wins*. Here we have a quote from Derek Fisher confirming this notion. Yes, the players know what gets them paid. And that means players are not just competing to win games, they are also competing with each other for shot attempts and ultimately salaries. This feature of the labor market, though, isn't about the league's collective bargaining agreement. It is really all about the NBA's confusion about what drives wins.

Of course—like the competitive balance story above—the link between scoring and pay has been discussed before. And like the competitive balance story above, one should expect that the link between scoring and pay will be discussed again.

"*Sports officials who stand to lose money from drug and other scandals won't work to expose the internal problems of their sport.*"

Athletes Are Getting Away with Doping

David Epstein

In the following viewpoint, David Epstein argues that much of the doping in professional and amateur sports goes undetected. He cites several reasons for his theory, including the difficulty of drug testing logistically and the lack of desire of sports officials to catch the perpetrators. The author's beliefs are backed by the steroid scandal that struck the MLB in the early 2000s, to which many believe the league turned a blind eye because the home run races believed to have been greatly caused by performance enhancing drugs inspired fans to flock to ballparks. But Epstein's premise that dopers are not being tracked and caught is debatable. Epstein has written about science, medicine, and sports science for Sports Illustrated *and* ProPublica.

As you read, consider the following questions:

1. Is the premise of the article that athletes get away with doping still viable in 2018?
2. What sport does the author indicate is most riddled with cheaters?
3. How does the author evaluate the US and international anti-drug Olympic organizations in their quest to create clean Olympic Games?

L ast week, we examined reasons why the very nature of drug testing technology—which cannot eliminate false positives and false negatives at the same time—means it will never be a perfect mechanism for catching cheaters. This may come as no big surprise to anyone who remembers the famous Nike commercial featuring video of Lance Armstrong taking a drug test. "What am I on?" Armstrong asks rhetorically. "I'm on my bike, busting my ass six hours a day." He was also on a raft of drugs, yet passed hundreds of tests. Certainly, testing technologically has progressed since then and will continue to do so. But even if technological holes are closed, logistical loopholes may remain. Here are four holes large enough for Lance to ride a bike through:

1. The Dog Was Eating My Homework ... While My Doorbell Was Broken

When athletes take small doses of synthetic hormones, the window during which they might fail a test is very short—often just hours. So it's critical that athletes don't know when the tests will occur. To facilitate year-round, unannounced testing of a limited number of top athletes, the World Anti-Doping Agency calls for "whereabouts requirements." Beginning in 2009, potential Olympians had to fill out forms letting anti-doping authorities know where they would be for at least one hour each day—between 6 a.m. and 11 p.m.—for the next few months. (An athlete's whereabouts calendar can be altered, and the US Anti-Doping Agency even has a mobile whereabouts app.) Still, athletes can miss three tests in 12 months before they face a sanction. It's only fair to give some wiggle room—any idea where you'll be three Tuesdays from now?—but it means athletes can sometimes avoid the testers by claiming to have stepped out briefly or that they didn't hear the doorbell. Or, as retired professional cyclist Tyler Hamilton—and admitted former doper—once succinctly summarized a low-tech method of chicanery: "We hid."

2. Testing Infrastructure? What Testing Infrastructure?

The World Anti-Doping Agency itself is not—as is commonly misunderstood—set up to drug test athletes around the world. WADA was launched just before the turn of the millennium to coordinate anti-doping efforts and rules around the world. The agency conducts research to better detect ever-more advanced doping, accredits labs that want to become certified for drug testing (and strips accreditations if labs don't maintain certain standards), and keeps the World Anti-Doping Code. The Code includes the list of banned substances and the methods and rules for how anti-doping efforts should be conducted by sports federations and countries. It was implemented before the 2004 Olympics and has been updated several times. So WADA simply keeps the Code; it's up to the Olympic committees, national and international sports federations, and anti-doping bodies in each individual country to actually implement it. Typically glacial bureaucratic movement has ensued. In one prominent instance, Renee Anne Shirley, former executive director of the Jamaica Anti-Doping Commission, pointed out that limited staff and expired testing kits led to a total halt to JADCO's out-of-competition testing in the three months before the 2012 London Olympics. (Athletes were still subject to testing by international governing bodies.) Implementing agreed upon anti-doping practices is still a fairly new and definitely evolving venture for plenty of countries and sports organizations, and it's still a global patchwork.

3. TUE

It's an abbreviation for "Tuesday" to you, but any athlete who sees those letters immediately thinks "therapeutic use exemption." Athletes have to be allowed to care for their health, and the TUE system allows them to apply for permission to use substances or medical procedures that would normally be restricted, ranging from corticosteroids and stimulants to IVs. The trouble is that any process by which athletes can gain permission to use potentially performance enhancing drugs also provides a possible anti-doping loophole. Perhaps the most stunning recent TUE revelation was that Yankees slugger Alex Rodriguez was actually given permission at one point to use synthetic testosterone, and then to use the drug clomiphene citrate, meant to boost testosterone in men who are not producing enough naturally. The Ultimate Fighting Championship also gave out a rash of exemptions for testosterone, with most athletes claiming they needed it because they had low testosterone for their age. In Olympic sports, an exemption for testosterone would be extraordinarily hard to come by. Simply low testosterone levels do not suffice; a rare condition—like being born without testicles or having them removed—would have to be present. But the prevalence of certain medications among athletes—like corticosteroids, both injected for pain and inhaled for asthma—has led some of the pros themselves to call for removal of the TUE process altogether, so that there would be no exemptions for otherwise restricted medication. As American distance runner Ben True recently put it: "I have a hard time with the idea that if you're that sick and need certain drugs that you're able to be at the top of the sport and race at the highest level. Maybe you just need to go home and rest and recover for a while."

4. Henhouse, Meet Fox

Officials at IAAF—track and field's international governing body—were understandably a tad defensive after a recent report by London's *Sunday Times* and German broadcaster ARD that a review of 12,000 leaked biological passport tests for track athletes from 2001 to 2012 found that around 15 percent of them were doping. The governing body has a lot to lose from the perception that cheating is rife and that many athletes get away with it. It falls in line with a host of recent scandals in pro sports in which the agency charged with rooting out cheaters was unsurprisingly "surprised." You didn't expect Sepp Blatter to lead the charge against corruption in World Cup soccer, did you? Or the UCI—cycling's governing body—to take down Lance Armstrong? Of course you didn't, just like you didn't expect Major League Baseball to interrupt the steroid-fueled home run chase—which propelled baseball back to relevance after a devastating strike—in order to bring you an important message about performance enhancing drugs.

Olympic sports are far better off than the MLBs of the world in this regard, as national anti-doping organizations—in America, the US Anti-Doping Agency, the folks who did bust Lance—do a lot of the heavy lifting. For example, they conduct out-of-competition testing, adjudicate violations, and even test foreign athletes who train in their countries. But sports federations themselves have a role as well, conducting in-competition testing (and some out-of-competition testing), educating athletes, and sanctioning rule violators. The irony, of course, is that the harder a sport attempts to police doping, the more commercial harm it suffers. A recent study found that the announcement of a performance enhancing drug violation in baseball temporarily reduces fan attendance. The NFL doesn't disclose the substance that a player tested positive for, so many football players who fail a test claim publicly that they forgot to get an exemption for their ADHD medication. So the NFL can never seem like it has an actual performance enhancing drug problem. It's a little like how the NHL stopped disclosing specific injuries (beyond "lower body injury" and "upper body injury") when concussions became a cause célèbre. That way fans aren't alerted to the frequency of concussions and the scope of the problem. It's the kind of behavior your local economist would predict: Sports officials who stand to lose money from drug and other scandals won't work to expose the internal problems of their sport. And as long as there are conflicts of interest in anti-doping, there are likely to be scandals akin to the reported cover-up of Russian runners' positive drug tests. Just last week, Lord Sebastian Coe was elected as the new president of the IAAF, and mentioned that conflicts of interest, both real and perceived, must be addressed. He then promptly drew criticism for making light of concerns over his own relationship with Nike—the biggest corporate name in the sport—for which he is a paid international ambassador. (Turns out Coe is also paid by a company that makes synthetic track surfaces, raising more questions over how serious he is about conflicts of interest.)

The good news is that the organizational and human problems are largely fixable, even while drug testing remains imperfect. The missed-tests provision could be tightened to allow fewer or even no misses, even if this meant that some athletes whose dogs actually were eating their homework when the drug testers showed up would surely be sanctioned. Perhaps a system mandating short suspensions for a single missed test would deter those who are intentionally avoiding anti-doping personnel while not excessively punishing those who have a legitimate excuse. Maybe there could even be a TUE-like system of applying for exemptions when a test is missed. Speaking of TUEs, that system could be tightened as well with more stringent evaluation of athletes' prescriptions. (And some athletes and national anti-doping organizations are calling for medications that don't require exemptions but that are widely used to gain a performance benefit—like thyroid hormone—to be restricted.) The tricky part in all of this is that it creates more logistical work and amplifies the off-the-field burden on athletes. And while athletes in Olympic sports must detail their whereabouts, requiring those in major pro sports—with powerful players' unions—to do the same is about as likely as the Jets winning the Super Bowl this year. So, as with testing technology in Olympic sports, the system is very far from perfect, but it's also the best one out there at the moment.

"*Female athletes work hard if not harder than their male counterparts to achieve an absolute target— especially in sports such as tennis and cricket.*"

Gender Pay Equity in Sports Is Only Fair

Kevin Netto

In the following viewpoint, Kevin Netto compares the physical differences in men and women to offer a scientifically based opinion on whether female athletes should be paid as much as their male counterparts. Without taking other factors into consideration, particularly the fact that male athletes in team sports draw significantly larger crowds, he concludes that female athletes should be paid the same as male athletes. The vast differences in outlook of Australian journalists and that of their American counterparts, who cover the NFL, NBA, and MLB, is evident here. One can certainly understand Netto's logic in regard to individual sports such as tennis and golf. Netto is an associate professor of physiotherapy and exercise science at Curtin University in Western Australia.

"Should Women Athletes Earn the Same as Men? The Science Says They Work as Hard," by Kevin Netto, The Conversation, April 18, 2016. https://theconversation.com/should-women-athletes-earn-the-same-as-men-the-science-says-they-work-as-hard-57210. Licensed under CC BY ND 4.0.

As you read, consider the following questions:

1. Based on his reasoning, should readers believe the author would conclude that WNBA players should make as much in salaries as their peers in the NBA?
2. Does the author's argument that women work harder to maximize their athletic potential make sense?
3. What sports does the author cite in making his points?

Should professional female athletes be paid the same as their male counterparts? It's a question that produces emotion, heated debate and a glaringly large glimpse into Pandora's Box.

We've had Novak Djokovic claim male tennis players should earn more because men's matches get more spectators. Women's bodies, he noted, "are much different than men's bodies. They have to go through a lot of different things that we don't have to go through. You know, the hormones and different stuff." After a public outcry he apologised for his comments.

Australia's women's soccer team, the Matildas, went on strike over the question of pay last year. In some recent good news, Cricket Australia's new pay deal for women will see its top female players become the highest paid team sports athletes in Australia, earning more than A$100,000 a year. Still, Steve Smith and a handful of the top ranked male players reportedly earn over A$2 million a season.

Most of the commentary we hear is just that, commentary. I'd like to approach the question of women, pay and sport from the perspective of exercise science.

Are female and male athletes physically different? You don't need a PhD to answer that one! But how does this affect performance in sport?

The biggest discrepancy in muscle distribution between a female and male body is that by and large, women have less muscle in the upper body (especially around the shoulders and neck) compared to men. The difference can be as large as 30 per cent in healthy individuals.

When applied to sport, the impact is clear. Let's compare the world record for a sport such as the javelin to that of the 100m sprint. The difference between the distance the javelin has been thrown in the men's and women's world records is around 30 per cent. The time difference between male and female athletes in the 100m sprint is about 10 per cent.

In sports such as javelin, tennis, golf or cricket, female athletes are substantially less strong and powerful in the upper body compared to their male counterparts.

For any given task in these sports, women have to work harder. To drive a golf ball 200 metres, for instance, a woman would need to use 80–90 per cent of her maximum force whereas a man might draw upon 60 per cent.

Ok, we get the biomechanics. How about the physiology?

Men have larger hearts (though some might argue the contrary); greater blood volume, more red blood cells, greater lung capacity and are on average, taller (15cm) and larger (10kg) than women.

The gap does narrow in athletic populations, but in terms of sports performance this means that for any given athletic task—such as running 100 metres in 11 seconds—a woman athlete would be using almost 100 per cent of her potential, whereas a male athlete might use 90 per cent of his potential to complete that goal.

There are exceptions, such as long distance swimming. Many women outswim men as a woman's greater fat mass allows better buoyancy and as such, more efficiency through the water.

However, in endurance and ultra-endurance land-based events, a male athlete's greater physiological potential has the upper hand.

Training Days

Another glaringly large difference between the sexes is the effect athletic training has on female and male bodies. Because of differences in sex hormones, male athletes have a greater response to training stimuli—such as weight training and strength and conditioning—compared to female athletes.

WOMEN'S SPORTS ARE VIRTUALLY IGNORED BY THE MEDIA

Anyone watching women win one third of all British medals in the 2012 Olympic games and elite sportswomen such as Jessica Ennis-Hill and Nicola Adams become household names would be forgiven for expecting the nation's newspapers to transform their coverage of women's sports in subsequent years. Yet a report out on Thursday shows how wrong anyone would be.

Research from Birmingham University reveals that six of our national newspapers actually produced fewer stories about women's sports a year on from the Olympics than they did before. In total, stories about men's sports outnumbered those about women's sports by 20 to one in March 2013 in six national titles—the *Sun*, *Mirror*, *Times*, *Telegraph*, *Mail* and *Express*.

Of 876 articles about sport in these newspapers during three weekends, 39 (4.5%), related to women's sport in February/March 2012, compared with 2.9% in 2013—not statistically significant until you reflect that 97% of sport coverage a year after the Olympic games was of men's sport. The amount of space given to those stories fell more significantly from 3.5% to 1.3% in 2013. (It proved

Male muscle tends to grow larger and stronger than female muscle, given comparable training regimes. This again points to differences in athletic potential.

These reasons are why most Olympic sports are divided (quite appropriately) by sex. In 2016, only equestrian and one sailing event (Nacra 17) will have mixed competitions, where men and women compete for medals on a equal basis.

The Injury Count

How about injury? Statistics show, in non-contact sports, that female athletes suffer more knee and shoulder injuries compared to males. This has been attributed to a wider pelvis (thus more impossible to find weekends without major men's sporting events and two of those weekends included home nations clashes in the rugby Six Nations championship, but with those sorts of percentages it can hardly have made much difference.)

Dr Claire Packer, a senior clinical lecturer in public health, who led the study said: "Maybe it was unrealistic to expect the 2012 games to solve the gender bias in reporting. It needs a much bigger policy push and a bigger effort to change people's behaviour within the media."

The argument usually put forward for the lack of coverage is that no one is interested in women's sport, yet the interest shown on social media and among TV viewers suggests otherwise. Women's football got its own series on BBC2 for a bit, while the women's football World Cup final of 2011 was at the time the most-tweeted event in the history of Twitter.

Previous research has shown that sports journalism has one of the lowest percentages of female journalists, with a Women in Journalism study three years ago revealing that just 3% of all sport stories in a given month were written by women.

"No Increase in Women's Sport Coverage Since the 2012 Olympics," by Jane Martinson, Guardian News and Media Limited, March 13, 2014.

knee injuries) and smaller muscle mass in the upper body (thus more shoulder injuries).

So for any given exposure to training or competition, female athletes are more at risk of injury. Needless to say, this would have dire impact on the earning potential of the individual.

On top of that statistic, here are a couple more interesting differences between the sexes. A woman's core body temperature can differ by up to 1°C from the mid-luteal to follicular phase of her menstrual cycle. Considering elevated core body temperature can be detrimental to athletic performance, a female athlete's physiology will be excessively stressed, especially competing in the heat compared to a male athlete who does not have these fluctuations.

And here's a curve ball for you. Females suffer more than two times more whiplash injuries in car accidents compared to males. Considering athletes spend time commuting to training and competition, female athletes are at 200 per cent greater risk of injuring their neck if even a minor car accident happens.

Again, the detriment to athletic performance and thus earning potential could be huge.

So should women athletes be paid the same as men? Obviously, there are other factors that might influence levels of pay beyond the amount of physical energy exerted.

Still, as a scientist, I deal with biomechanical and physiological facts. And these say female athletes work hard if not harder than their male counterparts to achieve an absolute target—especially in sports such as tennis and cricket.

They expose their bodies to similar, if not higher risks of injury, which could potentially be career ending.

Should they be remunerated equally? I think they should (yep, the scientist has an opinion) but I'll let the facts do the talking.

Periodical and Internet Sources Bibliography

The following articles have been selected to supplement the diverse views presented in this chapter.

Kurt Badenhausen, "Why No Women Rank Among the World's 100 Highest-Paid Athletes," *Forbes*, June 7, 2018. https://www.forbes .com/sites/kurtbadenhausen/2018/06/07/why-no-women-ranked -among-the-worlds-100-highest-paid-athletes/#36e6a10e3479.

Daniel Engber, "What If Doping Were Legal?," *Slate*, August 6, 2007. http://www.slate.com/articles/sports/sports_nut/2007/08/what _if_doping_were_legal.html.

Eldon L. Ham, "Pro Athletes Should Speak Out on Controversial Issues," *Sun-Sentinel* (Broward County, FL), January 12, 2015. http://www.sun-sentinel.com/opinion/commentary/os-ed -activist-athletes-front-burner-pro-20150112-story.html.

Bill Littlefield, "No Matter the Sport, Women Athletes Are Always Paid Less," Only a Game, April 16, 2016. http://www.wbur.org /onlyagame/2016/04/16/pay-gap-female-sports.

Gage McN., "Should Professional Athletes Have to Take Drug Tests?," Baruch College Campus HS Writing Magazine. https:// bcchswritingclass.wordpress.com/persuasive-essays/should- professional-athletes-have-to-take-drug-tests/.

Nichole M. Rens, "Changes in Fame and Fortune: A Phenomen- ological Study of Athletes Entering Retirement," UST Research Online, 2017. https://ir.stthomas.edu/cgi/viewcontent .cgi?article=1088&context=caps_ed_lead_docdiss.

Seattle Times, "NBA Changes Drug Testing Policy After Sonics Mishap," December 7, 2005. https://www.seattletimes.com /sports/nba-changes-drug-testing-policy-after-sonics-mishap/.

Matt Vasilogrambros, "When Athletes Take Political Stands," *Atlantic*, July 12, 2016. https://www.theatlantic.com/news /archive/2016/07/when-athletes-take-political-stands/490967/.

OPPOSING
VIEWPOINTS®
SERIES

CHAPTER 4

What Responsibility Do Team Owners Have to Their Players?

Chapter Preface

Sports franchise owners, of course, are first and foremost businesspeople. They may love the sport and the team they own, but above all they are investing in an opportunity to make money. But sports is unlike any other business in America, and it's not as simple as profit and loss. Sports franchises are a far greater part of the fabric of their cities than other such entities. When a local sports team moves out of a city, it does not merely tear the hearts out of loyal fans. It severely weakens area businesses such as hotels, bars, and restaurants. No other business in town attracts twenty thousand, thirty thousand, fifty thousand, even eighty thousand people on a nightly or weekly basis. Many people identify cities throughout America by their sports teams. Green Bay, Wisconsin, for instance, is known more as Packers country that anything else.

That is why it is frowned upon when owners pack up their teams and move to another location based on a perceived lack of support from their home base. Recent examples include the NBA team the Seattle SuperSonics and the NFL team the St. Louis Rams. That nonsupport, so to speak, does not mean there is a lack of fans in the stands. More likely it is the unwillingness of cities or the public itself to pay for new venues or upgrade existing ones. Many people have complained when owners refuse to pony up and spring for such initiatives themselves, then bolt to cities that will. Such was the case when Cleveland Browns owner Art Modell hightailed it to Baltimore despite weekly sellouts at the old Cleveland Stadium.

Some have suggested that the example of the Packers makes an ideal argument for city-owned sports franchises. Though millions of people through the United States and elsewhere care little about sports, it does not take a diehard fan to understand the economic importance of maintaining the existence of professional sports teams in their cities. The economic boon to businesses is undeniable, and such franchises can bring a town's community together like almost nothing else. For no other business can success inspire more than one million people to converge downtown to celebrate a champion. It is up to sports owners to understand the tie between their teams and the populace.

It is apparent that many of them simply do not. But what is the obligation of the team owner, given their rights in a capitalist system? As you will see in the following viewpoints, that is up for debate.

"A team belongs to more than just its owner. It belongs in a sense to its supporters, most especially those who buy the tickets and, increasingly, the taxpayers who provide lavish subsidies for the team's facilities."

Team Owners Are Guardians of Their Teams and Communities

Father Raymond J. de Souza

In the following viewpoint, Father Raymond J. de Souza argues that sports team owners need to understand their roles in the community and the fact that their responsibilities are unlike that of other business owners. The author asserts that the difference between sports team ownership and running other businesses is fandom. It is for that reason that owners have an obligation to their cities and to try their hardest to make the relationship between their franchisees and the cities in which they play work. De Souza is a Roman Catholic priest of the Archdiocese of Kingston, Ontario, Canada.

"Father Raymond J. de Souza: What Is the Role of Major-League Sports Team Owners?" by Father Raymond J. de Souza, National Post, September 27, 2012. Reprinted by permission.

As you read, consider the following questions:

1. What are the strongest points made by the author in arguing that owning a sports franchise carries with it special responsibilities?
2. Which legendary Canadian sports team does the author believe has recently failed its fans by putting out a mediocre product?
3. Which two major sports leagues does the author believe are failing the fans?

W ho owns a sports team? That is clear enough: the owner who bought it. He can do with it whatever he likes in accord with the policies of the league—i.e., the rules that all the owners establish together.

But to whom does a team belong? A team belongs to more than just its owner. It belongs in a sense to its supporters, most especially those who buy the tickets and, increasingly, the taxpayers who provide lavish subsidies for the team's facilities. It belongs to the wider community, too. No one throws a parade when ABC Widget Company has a record year; but entire cities celebrate sports championships.

Then there is a related question: Who owns the game? Certainly no owner of a single team owns the game, but does the league— meaning the consortium of owners—own the game? That would seem a step too far; a game is prior to any league, both ontologically and chronologically.

The pure ownership model seems rather inadequate in a week in which the conduct of professional sports leagues and owners has been subject to scathing criticism. There is the greatly unloved Gary Bettman, the NHL commissioner who has locked out the players—again. His mentor, David Stern, NBA commissioner, locked out the basketball players last season. Roger Goodell, NFL commissioner, locked out his players last year and is currently locking out the referees, resulting in a game that descended into total farce on Monday night. (The amount of money in dispute is less than the cost of a few Super Bowl commercials, but pigskin has been sacrificed to pigheadedness.)

To complete this sorry display, Edmonton Oilers owner Daryl Katz went to Seattle this week, musing about moving his team there unless the Edmonton city council adds tens of millions to the hundreds of millions that they have already promised him for a new arena. My *Post* colleague Kelly McParland called that rude, which was polite. The proper term for this effrontery is extortion, but it is so common in pro sports that it is considered mere negotiating.

The model simply does not fit the reality. A team owner is not like just another businessman, for a team is not just another business. Even basic economics recognizes this, for while all the owners of widget factories are in competition with each other, professional teams compete on the ice, but co-operate in the boardroom. A consortium of widget makers could not shut down the widget business in the way that the NHL can shut down professional hockey.

The simple commercial model does not fit sports teams. To be sure, there is plenty of commerce, but to think of team owners as purely commercial actors ignores their role as guardians of something greater—a team and its community, of the game itself. They are not just commercial actors; they are custodians.

In recent years, corporations have been encouraged to take account of not only their shareholders, but their "stakeholders" too. There are legal problems with this, as the fiduciary duty of directors is to the shareholders. Economically, it is not easy to distinguish between a stakeholder and a rent-seeker, or even a free rider. But the general sense of "stakeholder" duty is that a firm must take account of how its commercial activity affects third parties.

In the world of professional sports, though, the stakeholder model is clearly applicable. The shareholder model is obviously inadequate, which is why no one considers the Toronto Maple Leafs a successful team. Their shareholders profit mightily, but their stakeholders—let's call them "fans"—are offered a mediocre team. Fools they are, you might say, for handing over increasing sums for an inept team. Fair enough, but fan foolishness does not excuse failing custodianship.

The most elementary task of a custodian is to ensure that the game continues with honour and integrity. The NHL owners, and their fellow owners in the NFL, are failing as custodians. They likely consider themselves, as billionaires understandably might, commercially savvy. Being successful in business is admirable, but hardly rare. A more noble aspiration is to put commercial genius at the service of cultural guardianship, which is what sports is in large part about. The custodians of our games do not appear interested in any such service.

Failing as commercial operators ought to be embarrassing for those who own the NHL and NFL. Failing as custodians is a more grave matter, and they should be ashamed. We have discovered— again—that they are, to the contrary, utterly shameless.

| "The backlash against public funding
has caused MLS its own headaches for
stadiums that aren't using tax cuts."

The United States Is a Haven for Carpetbagging Sports Owners

Jakub Frankowicz

In the following viewpoint, Jakub Francowicz argues that one story coming from Major League Soccer (MLS) is rather alarming. The proposed move of the Columbus Crew to Austin, Texas, had been criticized greatly because its owner ignored the success of his current team simply because he had been given a sweeter deal in Texas. Such carpetbagging is not precedent setting, but Francowicz reports that it is unsettling nevertheless, since it leaves loyal Crew fans without a team despite their fine support and the significant success of their team on the field. Francowicz is is a freelance writer for the Guardian.

As you read, consider the following questions:

1. Why does the author think the Crew's story is inevitable?
2. Does the author here show bias in his view of the proposed move of the Columbus Crew to Austin?
3. What did Crew owner Anthony Precourt try to force the city of Columbus to do to keep its team?

"Where Can an Owner Move Their Football Club 1,000 Miles on a Whim? America," by Jakub Frankowicz, Guardian News and Media Limited, October 26, 2017. Reprinted by permission.

Coming off the United States' failure to qualify for the 2018 World Cup, Major League Soccer fans needed good news. What they got instead was a blindside.

Last week, *Sports Illustrated*'s Grant Wahl published a story detailing how Anthony Precourt, the California-based owner of Columbus Crew since 2013, had plans to move the team to Austin, Texas, over 1,000 miles away, in 2019. The stated purpose was to force the city of Columbus, Ohio, into giving the club a sweetheart tax deal on a new stadium in a downtown location. But the language of a press release from Columbus' front office made the move sound like a done deal.

In the release Precourt said that "despite our investments and efforts, the current course is not sustainable." MLS Commissioner Don Garber doesn't seem keen to stop any move either. "Crew SC is near the bottom of the League in all business metrics and the club's stadium is no longer competitive with other venues across MLS," he said in a statement. "The league is very reluctant to allow teams to relocate, but based on these factors, we support PSV's efforts to explore options outside of Columbus, including Austin, provided they find a suitable stadium." The surprise nature of the announcement is unusual for owners attempting to stay in their city, as they often encourage fans to influence their legislators to push a deal favorable to the club along. (On Tuesday, the mayor of Columbus revealed he had reached out to Precourt and Garber for meetings exploring options to keep the Crew in Columbus, which both accepted. The meetings are to take place in the coming weeks.)

The thought of one of MLS's founding clubs suddenly moving rattled the fans in the Nordecke, the supporters group coalition for the Crew. The Nordecke called for a #SavetheCrew Rally and they have enjoyed broad support from fans across the league.

It's easy to see why the developments may scare fans of other clubs, who could find themselves in a similar situation one day. Season ticket holders who wish to claim a refund will be able to do so until 3 November at 5pm ET. The faithful who are able to overcome the betrayal to attend a game in Austin would find themselves facing a 36-hour road trip or a $250, four-hour flight with at least one layover.

The news is remarkable for a team that was dominant from the mid- to late-2000s under the ownership of the Hunt Family. From 2004 to 2009 they won three Supporters' Shields, and added an MLS Cup to a Shield in 2008 for a double. There has been success more recently too. Since Precourt took over, the Crew made the 2015 MLS Cup final, where they lost 2–1 to the Portland Timbers. This season, they finished fifth in the Eastern Conference and made the playoffs.

While Columbus's Mapfre Stadium, the supposed focus of Precourt's decision to move is hardly Camp Nou, it was only built in 1999. And the stadium is something of a sacred site. It was the first soccer-specific-stadium in MLS history and laid out a blueprint for financial feasibility, leading the league out of situations in which teams played in huge, largely empty, NFL arenas. It is also the home of arguably the most memorable matches in US soccer history. After losses to Mexico in the US to largely pro-Mexico crowds, US Soccer took a chance on the stadium and the city's ability to sell out the game in frigid temperatures for a true home field advantage. The result was the beginning of a US soccer legend, a string of four World Cup Qualifiers against Mexico that ended as 2–0 victories, entering the phrase "Dos a Cero" into American Soccer fans' lexicon.

Of course, teams moving in US sports is by no means new. In the past two years in the NFL alone, the Rams have relocated from St Louis to Los Angeles, the Chargers from San Diego to Los Angeles, and the Raiders will move from Oakland to Las Vegas. The NBA also moved the SuperSonics from Seattle to Oklahoma City in 2008, and rebranded them as the Thunder. And the MLS itself has moved the San Jose Earthquakes to Houston and changed their name to the Dynamo after the end of the 2005 season, but San Jose would gain its team back in time to begin play in 2008 as part of MLS expansion.

It's easy to see why Precourt wants to move. According to *Forbes*, Crew are valued at $130m, lower than any other MLS franchise. A move to Austin, one of the United States' fastest growing cities—and a city without an NBA, NFL, NHL or MLB team—would instantly boost its valuation.

There's no guarantee that there's an appetite for an MLS team in the college sports crazed city where the University of Texas Longhorns reign supreme. But maybe it doesn't matter, and Precourt is looking to pull a move similar to Dean Spanos, who is said to have upped the value of his Chargers team by a minimum of $500m simply by moving his team from San Diego to the more attractive market of Los Angeles despite their failure to properly fill the Stubhub Center, where the Los Angeles Galaxy are the primary tenants.

Perhaps MLS felt insulated from this as part of soccer, where team moves are so rare that almost everybody who follows soccer knows the name of MK Dons for the club's 2003 move from Wimbledon to Milton Keyes.

Or perhaps it's because MLS has always seemed progressive, if only because its fans have been. It's not uncommon to go to a match and see an assortment of flags in the supporters sections championing LGBT Pride, Black Lives Matter, and other progressive movements. While some stadiums have removed these flags, the enforcement of what qualifies as too political seems to be left up to the front offices of the clubs themselves. Notably, MLS was home to the first openly gay professional athlete playing on the field in the US, Robbie Rogers. Now MLS has made it clear that it supports progressive values only as far as they help their checkbook.

And maybe soccer fans should have seen it coming. The MLS owners have continued an American tradition, despite overwhelming evidence publicly funded stadiums are a poor investment, as John Oliver memorably explained. The backlash against public funding has caused MLS its own headaches for stadiums that aren't using tax cuts. Miami has been slow to warm to David Beckham's forever-coming-soon team despite a private-funding promise after the nightmare of Marlins' Ballpark financing. In that instance, Miami-Dade County pitched in $500m to construct that stadium, money they took loans out to get and will eventually cost the county billions.

Even deals that are in the team's favor don't always ensure compliance down the road. In the years following the opening of Red Bull Arena, the Red Bull organization failed to pay dues on land that the small town of Harrison, New Jersey, had purchased for them at the cost of $40m to the town. Millions of dollars in back taxes were owed, and a compromise came years later. The area's regeneration that Red Bull promised is still incomplete with empty lots dotting the landscape around the stadium.

With all this history, there's a sense of inevitability to the Crew's story. The Crew fans will protest, MLS fans everywhere will join in. The city of Columbus won't and shouldn't give in, and in all likelihood, the move to Austin was finished before fans knew about it. FC Cincinnati—who average crowds of more than 20,000 in the second-tier USL—will likely be one of the league's next expansion choices, and Garber will offer that as an MLS "return" to Ohio. And eventually the league will feel like that's the way it always was. But the era of innocence in MLS will be over.

> *"The NFL owners ... [are] free to establish any policies they like, and they like their 'no community ownership' rule because it benefits them financially, local fans be damned."*

US Sports Leagues Are Given Too Much Latitude

Ken Reed

In the following viewpoint, Ken Reed takes the NFL to task after a spate of franchise relocations as San Diego and St. Louis lost their teams. Reed is angered by what he perceives as a league creating its own rules as a monopoly and preventing cities from owning their own franchises because it does not allow owners and the league to maximize profits. He believes that such policies alienate fans, even in cities that have given tremendous support. Reed is sports policy director for League of Fans, a sports reform project, and author of Ego vs. Soul in Sports.

As you read, consider the following questions:

1. How does the author explain his view that the NFL has a monopoly?
2. What community-owned NFL team does the author cite in claiming such an arrangement can work?
3. What longtime consumer advocate offers his view of NFL relocations in the viewpoint?

"NFL's Relocation Game Screws Fans," by Ken Reed, Ken Reed, January 20, 2016. Reprinted by permission.

While watching the recent NFL relocation charade involving the Rams, Chargers and Raiders play out, I was reminded once again that the fundamental problem in professional sports is that each sport is a self-regulated monopoly. Our pro sports leagues—and the franchise owners within—have basically been given free reign in the United States.

As a result, our old friends ego and greed are driving policymaking and decision-making in pro sports. A profit-at-all-costs (PAAC) mentality is at the root of virtually every action taken by pro sports owners. The results are seldom pretty for fans.

Consider that despite the fact the Rams have been playing in a fully functional domed stadium paid for by the taxpayers of St. Louis—one which taxpayers are still paying for—the Rams have apparently decided to move to greener (as in money) pastures in Los Angeles.

The Rams are leaving St. Louis while local citizens still owe more than $100 million in debt on the bonds used to build the sports palace the team has been making huge profits in.

This isn't uncommon, as sports journalist Dave Zirin points out.

"In the United States, we socialize the debt of sports and privatize the profits," says Zirin.

NFL owners (and those in our other major professional sports leagues) are unencumbered when it comes to their cartel practices. They do not have to deal with the checks and balances of an open marketplace, or the oversight of public regulation agencies, as do other monopolistic industries in the United States.

It's a system that needs changing. Our top priority should be the concerns of the millions of fans that have made the NFL so popular, not the greedy concerns of a few billionaire owners.

There is a better way, and there is an example in place.

"The self-regulated monopoly system in pro sports—including anti-trust exemptions—allows owners to pursue a profit-at-all-costs agenda at the expense of fans," says consumer advocate Ralph Nader. "This system has resulted in owners playing one city off another in the quest for new taxpayer-funded stadiums and other freeloading. A community ownership model, like the Green Bay Packers', works. It's a better way to structure and administer professional sports. It should become an optional mainstay of sports policy in this country."

The best town in pro sports is also the smallest: Green Bay, Wisconsin, home of the Packers.

The Green Bay Packers are owned by the fans, not a wealthy owner/corporation operating with a PAAC philosophy. The Packers are a publicly-owned non-profit with a unique stock ownership structure.

The team issued stock to the public in 1923 in order to stay afloat as a franchise. Ownership pays no dividends and doesn't provide any other perks. (Most notably, there aren't any game ticket privileges!) The Packers have conducted a few additional rounds of stock sales since 1923. Today, the franchise has 112,158 shareholders who own 4.7 million shares. Most shareholders live in the Green Bay area, or at least the state of Wisconsin, although there are no residency requirements. Nevertheless, all profits are invested back into the team, and as a community-owned franchise, the team won't be leaving Green Bay.

Green Bay's bylaws state that the Packers are "a community project, intended to promote community welfare." What a refreshing concept.

"It makes them an example," according to sports and culture writer Patrick Hruby. "A case study. A working model for a better way to organize and administer pro sports."

What would the NFL have looked like if every franchise had been owned through a Packers-like model since 1960?

"The upshot?" asks Hruby. "Had the Baltimore Colts' ownership structure been similar to Green Bay's, they never would have left in overnight trucks for Indianapolis. The Cleveland Browns never would have left for Baltimore. The Seattle Sonics never would have jetted to Oklahoma City."

And today, fans in St. Louis, San Diego and Oakland wouldn't be worried about losing their teams to other cities.

Yes, the reason St. Louis had the Rams in the first place was because the franchise left Los Angeles to come to St. Louis to play in St. Louis' new taxpayer-financed stadium. But the reason St. Louis citizens had to build the new stadium was to lure an NFL franchise back to town after the Cardinals packed up and left St. Louis for Arizona.

It's a crazy system, one that screws football fans and taxpayers and only benefits a handful of billionaire franchise owners.

The Green Bay model is a better way.

"Green Bay is a dangerous example for [sports] owners," contends Zirin. "Because the franchise proves the argument for public ownership in practice."

Michael N. Danielson, in his book *Home Team: Professional Sports and the American Metropolis*, writes, "Professional team sports in the United States and Canada have always been rooted in places. Major league teams have fostered close identification with the urban areas where they played, and sports fans are primarily interested in the fortunes of their home team …"

Due to the close identification a city's fans have with their local teams and the prestige and civic self-esteem that pro sports franchises can sometimes bring a community, the stakes are high for cities when they play the "pro sports game." Cities compete for the limited number of pro sports teams available. They fight to acquire sports franchises and make a concerted effort to protect the ones they currently have.

"Threats to relocate arouse public concern largely because of the emotional and symbolic connections between teams, places and people," according to Danielson.

As a result, for the last half-century, pro sports' wealthy owners have taken advantage of the economic and political advantages we've given them as a society, along with the loyalty and close identification fans have with pro sports franchises, to secure new sports palaces with little out-of-pocket expense on their part.

The clear answer to this situation is community ownership. However, decades ago, pro sports owners recognized the threat that community ownership represented to their golden goose and took steps against community ownership.

In fact, in the NFL, former commissioner Pete Rozelle changed the NFL constitution in 1960 in order to prevent another Green Bay Packers ownership situation. Article V, Section 4 of the NFL constitution, also known as the "Green Bay Rule," says that "charitable organizations and/or corporations not organized for profit and not now a member of the league may not hold membership in the National Football League."

The NFL owners have said no to community ownership because they can. They're free to establish any policies they like, and they like their "no community ownership" rule because it benefits them financially, local fans be damned. They're a self-regulated monopoly; blessed by our government with great profits. (Who has a better deal in America than NFL owners?)

It stinks for pro sports fans. Congress needs to step in and rectify the situation. Lord knows the NFL's self-regulated, greed-driven owners won't do it on their own.

> *"Because League policy favors stable team community relations, clubs are obligated to work diligently and in good faith to obtain and to maintain suitable stadium facilities in their home territories."*

NFL Regulation of Team Relocation Is an Uphill Battle

Beau Lynott

In the following viewpoint, Beau Lynott argues that his city followed all the criteria required to maintain its franchise as it weighed numerous proposals to build a new stadium for the San Diego Chargers. In the end, however, the team moved to Los Angeles, a city that already had an NFL team. This transfer absolutely crushed Chargers fans. The author cites the NFL Constitution and Bylaws and its Policies and Procedures for Proposed Relocation to make his case. He expresses his hope that the league would block the move, but as we know now, it didn't happen. Lynott is a contributor to Voice of San Diego.

"How the NFL Regulates Franchise Relocation (or Tries To)," by Beau Lynott, Voice of San Diego, February 24, 2015. Reprinted by permission.

As you read, consider the following questions:

1. When did the lease for Qualcomm Stadium in San Diego end?
2. Does the author believe the Chargers worked in good faith with the NFL to ensure they would stay in San Diego?
3. At the time this viewpoint was written, what was the last NFL team to relocate?

B y now you've heard about the Chargers' stunning partnership with their arch-rival Oakland Raiders to build a $1.7 billion (!) stadium in Carson, south of Los Angeles.

There have been a lot of stadium agreements and plans in L.A. over the last 20 years. None has been realized. It's different this time, we're told, even though the Chargers have played footsie with Carson before.

It's worth reviewing, then, how the NFL regulates the relocation of its franchises.

The NFL's Constitution and Bylaws, in Article IV, Section 3, states:

> No member club shall have the right to transfer its franchise or playing site to a different city, either within or outside its home territory, without prior approval by the affirmative vote of three-fourths of the existing member clubs of the League.

Teams can next apply for relocation between Jan. 1 and Feb. 15, 2016. With 75 percent of the league's 32 teams needed for approval, it would take nine "no" votes to deny a move.

No team has switched cites since 1997, when the Houston Oilers moved to Tennessee and later became the Titans. That move came on the heels of the Cleveland Browns' "transfer" to Baltimore in 1996, and after the Rams and Raiders left Los Angeles (Anaheim in the Rams' case) in 1995.

Twenty years later the battle for L.A. (or the battle to use L.A. as leverage) is officially on.

Which raises the question of whether the NFL can, or would, prevent a team from moving.

The Raiders became the most notorious contradiction of the league's ability to do so when they moved to Los Angeles in 1982, via court battle over the unanimous objection of league owners.

The one instance of the modern-era NFL successfully blocking a move came in 1996, when then-Seattle Seahawks owner Ken Behring shipped the team's equipment to Anaheim in an attempt to seize the abandoned Los Angeles market.

That was a unique situation. The team had nine years remaining on its stadium lease. The league was wary of abandoning yet another market after the relocations of the Rams, Raiders and Browns. NFL officials threatened the Seahawks with sanctions and county officials obtained a restraining order to prevent the team from relocating.

Behring returned the team to Seattle and later agreed to sell the franchise to a local buyer.

No such scenario exists for the teams currently flirting with Los Angeles. The Raiders, Rams and Chargers are each on terminable leases in their current homes.

The Chargers' lease at city-owned Qualcomm Stadium runs through 2020, but the team can get out of the lease between February 1 and May 1 of each year. The lease termination fee decreases on a sliding scale, with the team owing the city of San Diego a little over $15 million if it decides to skip town in 2016.

(Incidentally, that is not enough to pay off the debt the city still owes on the stadium renovation from 1997. The city owes $57 million and will make payments on it until 2026. This year, the payment is $4.8 million.)

Before the big Chargers-Raiders announcement, the NFL attempted to reassert its authority over franchise movement, and of the Los Angeles market specifically.

WHO SHOULD PAY?

With the news that the NFL approved the Raiders' move from Oakland to Las Vegas, there are now THREE teams (Raiders, Rams and Chargers) heading to new digs within a couple of years of each other. The driver behind all three moves is new stadium facilities to provide a higher quality venue and increased revenue opportunities.

At least one NFL owner feels that the public shouldn't be shouldering the costs, that the teams should pay for new stadiums and improvements to existing stadiums.

ESPN reports:

The only owner to vote against the Raiders moving to Las Vegas, Miami Dolphins owner Stephen Ross told reporters here on Monday that he believes Raiders owner Mark Davis did not use all of his options to get a stadium deal done in Oakland.

Owners voted 31–1 to approve the Raiders application to relocate to Las Vegas. The Raiders received an unprecedented $750 million in public money to build a new stadium for the team. Ross, who voted against the project, recently paid for over $500 million in stadium improvements at Hard Rock Stadium—

After the January announcement of Rams owner Stan Kroenke's plans to build a stadium in Inglewood, Pittsburgh Steelers owner Art Rooney II said the Rams still had to follow the rules of relocation.

"That's why we have league committees and approval processes," he told the *Los Angeles Times*. "I think we're comfortable that we could stop a team legally from moving if it didn't go through the process."

Still, the league hasn't maintained unanimity. Rooney's statements came in response to Dallas Cowboys owner Jerry Jones saying the Rams could simply choose to move without league approval.

The league tried to further maintain control of the L.A. market by establishing a committee that would study and coordinate any moves to Southern California.

the home for the Dolphins—and believes owners should foot the bill for new stadiums in their markets rather than asking for public money.

"You've got to look around," Ross said. "There's very little public money available for teams today. And if you own a team, you should have the deep pockets to deliver. You need some public money for infrastructure and things like that. But with the costs of stadiums today, our country can't afford to put all of the money in those things."

Including this $750 million for the Raiders new home in Las Vegas, nearly $7 billion of public funding has fueled the development of 21 stadiums and three major renovations in the last couple of decades.

That oughta do it. The NFL's two-decade blitz of stadium development largely ended this week with the granddaddy of them all: a nearly $1 billion gift from the tax coffers of Nevada to lure the Oakland Raiders to Las Vegas for the 2020 season.

"Should NFL Teams Pay for Their Stadiums?" by Capt Ron, Vox Media, March 28, 2017.

So, under what criteria could the NFL actually keep a team from moving?

The NFL's Policy and Procedures for Proposed Franchise Relocation states:

Article 4.3 confirms that each club's primary obligation to the League and to all other member clubs is to advance the interests of the League in its home territory. This primary obligation includes, but is not limited to, maximizing fan support, including attendance, in its home territory. Article 4.3 also confirms that no club has an "entitlement" to relocate simply because it perceives an opportunity for enhanced club revenues in another location. Indeed, League traditions disfavor relocations if a club has been well-supported and financially successful and is expected to remain so.

Teams aren't supposed to just pick up and move simply because the cash looks greener elsewhere:

> Because League policy favors stable team community relations, clubs are obligated to work diligently and in good faith to obtain and to maintain suitable stadium facilities in their home territories, and to operate in a manner that maximizes fan support in their current home.

The Chargers would be regarded as having fulfilled this obligation to the letter, with their oft-repeated mantra of "we've made nine stadium proposals in 14 years" in San Diego.

The policies and procedures list 12 "Factors That May Be Considered In Evaluating The Proposed Transfer" of a team to a new city. None would appear to bar a potential Chargers relocation. Particularly the following:

> The adequacy of the stadium in which the club played its home games in the previous season; the willingness of the stadium authority or the community to remedy any deficiencies in or to replace such facility, including whether there are legislative or referenda proposals pending to address these issues; and the characteristics of the stadium in the proposed new community.

Mayor Kevin Faulconer has agreed to speed up his stadium task force's timeline, but so far no actual plan exists. The dilapidated condition of Qualcomm Stadium and the team's long crusade for a new stadium bode well for the Chargers.

Again, the Rams might just move to L.A. anyway and beat the Chargers out of their leverage. Assuming the Rams, or the Chargers and Raiders, or some combination of the three, actually applies and is approved to relocate, what will it cost them?

Franchises that moved in the past were charged a relocation fee. The Oilers paid $28 million for their move to Tennessee, and the Rams $29 million to move to St. Louis.

The numbers most commonly thrown around for an L.A. relocation fee range from $250–$500 million.

Finally, would the Chargers-Raiders stadium in Carson be eligible for a loan of up to $200 million from the NFL? Both teams reportedly expect to receive loans of $200 million each from the NFL stadium fund. A league spokesman said, "A stadium project can be eligible for league financing provided the project and its sponsors meet certain criteria. A Carson project would be eligible and could apply if it met those criteria." But stadium researcher Neil deMause points out that the league's G-4 lending criteria requires "the project must not involve any relocation of or change in an affected club's 'home territory.'"

The NFL defines "home territory" as:

> the city in which such club is located and for which it holds a franchise and plays its home games and includes the surrounding territory to the extent of 75 miles in every direction from the exterior corporate limits of such city.

Logic dictates, and as any diehard Chargers fan will tell you, that Carson is not home territory.

> *"No league is voluntarily going to allow its franchises to fall into public hands when it can keep on using its monopoly power over team ownership to extract subsidies."*

Local Governments Should Buy the Franchise Instead of the Stadium

Neil deMause

In the following viewpoint, Neil deMause argues for the need for city-owned franchises. The author maintains that he understands the difficulty in executing such a solution to carpetbagging, particularly in the NFL, which he states owns a monopoly and yearns to earn subsidies from all its teams. DeMause believes only by taking extreme measures can the fan bases in NFL cities feel that their franchises are safe from carpetbagging owners that ignore even the finest support in attempts to relocate teams to cities that give them the best stadium and lease deals. In sports parlance, "carpetbagging" refers to athletes switching teams or teams switching cities to take advantage of economic opportunity. DeMause is a Brooklyn-based freelance journalist who writes for books, magazines, and newspapers.

"The Radical Case for Cities Buying Sports Teams, Not Sports Stadiums," by Neil deMause, Vice Sports, December 29, 2014. Reprinted by permission.

As you read, consider the following questions:

1. Just how offbeat is the solution to rampant relocation offered by Neil deMause in this viewpoint?
2. What sports leagues besides the NFL does the author cite in making his case for change?
3. How strong is the case made in the viewpoint in favor of municipally owned big-league sports teams?

When the Washington, D.C. city council unanimously approved spending $183 million in cash and tax breaks on a new stadium for D.C. United earlier this month, reactions were split, to say the least. Some in the media celebrated a long-awaited deal to give the 18-year-old Major League Soccer franchise its own soccer-specific stadium for the first time as crucial to keeping the team from leaving the District, while revitalizing an underdeveloped neighborhood. Others (including, yes, me and *VICE*'s Aaron Gordon) pointed to the fact that this would be the largest public subsidy ever for an MLS franchise, that the company that wrote the economic impact report later admitted that its rosy estimates were overblown, and that soccer stadiums have never been known to revitalize squat, anyway.

And then there were those who wondered: for $183 million, wouldn't it have been cheaper for D.C. to skip the stadium and just buy the team?

It's an especially cogent question with D.C. United, since MLS teams haven't historically come with crazy high price tags. Indonesian media mogul Erick Thohir and sports-agent-turned-NBA-exec Jason Levien paid $30 million for 60 percent of the team two years ago, putting the valuation of the whole franchise at a then-MLS-record $50 million. Yes, some teams have changed hands for more since then—most notably, the owners of Manchester City paid $100 million for the rights to an expansion New York franchise, NYC F.C., that will begin play next spring. But even then, for what it's paying for a stadium, D.C. could have gotten the whole team and all its future revenues, plus had enough left over for either David Luiz or for keeping 5,000 city residents from becoming homeless, take your pick.

And this isn't an uncommon scenario. The city of Miami and Dade County spent more than $800 million in 2009 on a new stadium for the Marlins, who according to *Forbes'* estimates could have been had at the time, lock, stock, and Hanley Ramirez, for just $277 million. Last year, Glendale, Arizona approved $225 million in operating subsidies for the Coyotes—this on top of the arena the city had already provided to the team—to grease the skids so that new owners could buy the team for $170 million. And mere blocks from the site of the new D.C. United stadium, the Washington Nationals received about $700 million in taxpayer money for their new stadium, even as the team itself was being sold for $450 million.

The numbers make your eyes glaze over after a bit, but add them up and you get all kinds of crazy. If the goal of fronting cash for new sports venues is to keep team owners from using their monopoly-given right to skip town and leave fans with no one to root for, then one workaround is obvious: cut out the middleman, and buy the team.

If you're thinking, Wait, my local government can't even pick up the garbage on time, what would it look like if they had to hold six months of hearings to decide on whether to sign a shortstop?, there's actually plenty of precedent for this, none of it bad. Several minor-league baseball teams are or have been municipally owned, and manage their operations the same way any billionaire who decides to buy a team as a plaything does: they hire professional managers to run the day-to-day show. A similar mechanism is in place for the three Canadian Football League franchises that are owned by fans via non-profit corporations (a la the Green Bay Packers), not to mention many of Europe's top soccer teams, including the last two European Champions League winners, Real Madrid and Bayern Munich.

Okay, so there is one small holdup with the public owning sports teams in the US, which is that the major pro sports leagues here have dedicated themselves to blocking it at every turn. McDonald's heiress Joan Kroc once tried to give the Padres to the city of San Diego as a charitable donation, but was overruled by MLB; a similar league edict later prevented the city of Pittsburgh from getting a share of the Pirates in exchange for a $20 million "loan" that was never repaid. The NFL was so freaked by the mere prospect of anyone trying to replicate the Packers that it wrote a ban on non-profit ownership into its league constitution. Congress considered a bill to pull leagues' antitrust exemption for TV rights if they barred community ownership, but like just about all Congressional attempts to reign in sports leagues, it's gone nowhere.

Okay, so no league is voluntarily going to allow its franchises to fall into public hands when it can keep on using its monopoly power over team ownership to extract subsidies. Is there any other way to force them to?

The answer is: maybe. And the trick lies in one of the same governmental powers that team owners use on their side in stadium deals: the power of eminent domain.

You're probably familiar with eminent domain as the means by which the government forcibly takes private land to make way for a highway or public building or hyperspace bypass, having only to pay whatever a court decides after the fact to be fair market value. The legal principle goes back hundreds of years, and doesn't have a great rep, especially as courts have expanded the notion of "public use" to include taking people's houses to hand over to private developers so long as it would promote "economic development"—even if there was no guarantee that the development would stick around more than a few years.

In the eyes of the courts, though, there should be no legal difference between a few acres of dirt and other private property such as, say, a pro sports franchise. Back in the dim recesses of sports history, the city of Oakland and state of Maryland attempted to test this theory, launching condemnation proceedings against the Raiders and Colts to try to block those teams' moves to Los Angeles and Indianapolis in the 1980s. Both were unsuccessful, for different reasons: in the Colts case, a court ruled that the state had acted too late, signing the eminent domain bill into law hours after Colts owner Robert Irsay, seeing what was coming, had packed the team's entire worldly goods into moving vans and sent them to Indianapolis (via 15 different highways, to avoid arousing suspicion). The Raiders case, meanwhile, bounced around the courts for a while before an appeals judge ruled that seizing the team would unfairly interfere with interstate commerce. (Yes, Oakland and L.A. are both in the same state, but the NFL is interstate, and … something about the Commerce Clause, okay?)

And as far as legal precedents go, that's been it for the past 30 years. Roger Noll, the Stanford economist who's followed franchise relocations for so long that he actually testified against Bud Selig's attempt to duck taxes for buying the Seattle Pilots and moving them to Milwaukee, says that "whether eminent domain would work probably varies from state to state and from judge to judge. In the past two decades the courts have become more skeptical of the use of eminent domain and so have narrowed its scope, but this use probably is still in the range of uncertainty."

Noll says—and David Morris of the Institute for Local Self-Reliance, which has advocated for public ownership of sports teams, agrees—that the bigger problem these days would likely be cost. Franchise values, floated by the cable TV bubble, have soared in recent years to where a United or Marlins situation is less likely—especially if courts require that taxpayers pay a premium in order to buy a team.

Still, eminent domain can be a worthwhile arrow in the municipal quiver. Say you're a city council with a pro sports team demanding $200 million or so in public cash for a new building—let's call them the "Milwaukee Bucks"—under threat of leaving town if its owners' demands aren't met. Instead of reaching for your municipal checkbook, you respond by drawing up eminent domain paperwork.

In the best case scenario, the mere threat is enough to force the team owners to lower their subsidy demands. In the worst, yes, you're stuck paying close to $600 million for an NBA franchise, but keep in mind two things: first off, that's how much the current Bucks owners just paid on the open market for the franchise, so presumably somebody thinks they'll bring in enough revenue to make that worthwhile. Plus, if you don't want to be stuck with the risk of the Bucks not earning back your investment, you can always re-sell the team to new private investors—even if you need to sell for $50 million or $100 million less in order to get new owners to agree to an ironclad lease, that's still cheaper than handing over $200 million for nothing.

Is that all too glib to be politically palatable? Maybe. But if there's one thing that we've seen time and again, it's that elected officials are—with a few notable exception—way too timid about exploring what cards they have to play in stadium and arena battles. As Chicago White Sox owner Jerry Reinsdorf famously said after threatening to move his team to Florida in order to extract stadium money from the Illinois legislature, "a savvy negotiator creates leverage." There's nothing stopping cities from trying to be a little savvy, too.

> *"Amid all the jockeying, a decades-long debate rages on: Does it make economic sense for cities and states to use public money to build sports facilities?"*

Why Should Public Money Be Used to Build Stadiums?

Elaine S. Povich

In the following viewpoint, Elaine S. Povich argues that the economic boon and individual worker benefits promised when public money is used to build stadiums simply does not exist. Povich cites examples of such arrangements that did not prove financially beneficial to the cities or their employment situations. She indicates that owners yearning to upgrade existing venues or have new ones built should use their own funds or raise money through other means. The use of public money to build stadiums and arenas has been criticized by many who state that such funds could be used to help people far more needy than sports team owners. Povich covers consumer affairs for Stateline, *a project sponsored by the Pew Charitable Trusts.*

"Amid Building Boom, Debate over Publicly Funded Stadiums Goes On," by Elaine S. Povich, NewsHour Productions LLC, July 13, 2016. Reprinted by permission.

As you read, consider the following questions:

1. What specific examples does Povich use here to argue that using public money to build stadiums is a bad idea?

2. Does the author here indicate that team owners are wealthy enough to fund new stadiums or arenas themselves?

3. Why does Povich evoke the name of former president Barack Obama in this article?

Missouri and St. Louis tried mightily to keep the NFL Rams from decamping for Los Angeles, offering $400 million in state and city money for a new stadium. To justify the public expense, officials argued that the team, which moved from Los Angeles to St. Louis two decades ago, was an economic engine for the region.

They offered to put up the money even though the Rams' billionaire owner, Stan Kroenke, could afford to build a new stadium on his own. Ultimately, Kroenke opted to do just that, announcing in January that he would spend $1.9 billion of his own fortune to build a new stadium for the Rams in Inglewood, southwest of downtown Los Angeles.

Two other NFL teams, the San Diego Chargers and the Oakland Raiders, also are eyeing a move to the nation's second largest city. But Nevada is hoping to grab the Raiders for itself, by dangling a $1.4 billion stadium that would be paid for, at least in part, by the taxpayers. Meanwhile in Atlanta, construction is underway on a new $950 million stadium for the NFL Falcons, to be financed partly through bonds secured by extending a tax on hotel and motel rooms.

Amid all the jockeying, a decadeslong debate rages on: Does it make economic sense for cities and states to use public money to build sports facilities?

As soon as the Rams-Inglewood deal was announced, Moody's Investment Service said the move would boost Inglewood's sagging economy.

"The new stadium will likely inject thousands of jobs into the local economy during the construction phase, as well as many new jobs post-completion," Moody's said. Inglewood will gain $18.7 million to $28 million of new annual revenue over 16 years, according to Moody's.

In Atlanta, where the city and Fulton County decided to direct proceeds from a 7 percent hotel-motel tax to pay the debt service on municipal bonds that are financing Mercedes-Benz Stadium, officials are predicting a similar impact. The NFL also selected the city and its future stadium to host the 2019 Super Bowl.

"Being honored with the [Super Bowl] is proof positive that public-private partnerships in the area of urban development can result in constructive outcomes," Atlanta City Council President Ceasar Mitchell said in a statement in May, when the NFL selected the site. "I applaud the collaborative efforts of the leadership team that made this a reality and look forward to hosting Super Bowl 53 like only Atlanta can."

But many economists maintain that states and cities that help pay for new stadiums and arenas rarely get their money's worth. Teams tout new jobs created by the arenas but construction jobs are temporary, and ushers and concession workers work far less than 40 hours a week.

Furthermore, when local and state governments agree to pony up money for stadiums, taxpayers are on the hook for years—sometimes even after the team leaves town. St. Louis, for example, is still paying $6 million a year on debt from building the Edward Jones Dome, the old home of the Rams that opened in 1995, despite the team's move to California. The debt is financed by a hotel tax and taxes on "game day" revenues like concessions and parking.

Jackson Brainerd, a research analyst at the National Conference of State Legislatures (NCSL), said the teams often hold up cities and states for sweet financing deals by threatening to move.

"Clearly major league professional sports teams are all fully capable of paying for stadiums themselves," he said, citing Los Angeles.

Tax-Free Bonds

Governmental entities have long used tax-free municipal bonds to finance infrastructure projects, including sports stadiums. Investors buy the bonds as a relatively risk-free vehicle to earn interest. Although the bonds generally pay lower interest rates to the buyer, they are attractive because of their tax-free status.

In his 2016 budget, President Barack Obama proposed getting rid of tax-free bonds to help finance stadiums, a practice that costs the US Treasury $146 million a year, according to a 2012 Bloomberg analysis. Bloomberg calculated that the $17 billion in tax-exempt debt used to build stadiums since 1986 would cost taxpayers $4 billion. The idea, like most of Obama's budget, failed to gain traction in the Republican-dominated Congress.

As far back as the Tax Reform Act of 1986, the government has tried to limit public financing of stadiums, arguing that the stadiums—unlike other publicly funded infrastructure like roads and bridges—only serve a small number of people and that rich team owners should foot the bill. The tax reform measure included a provision prohibiting direct stadium revenue—such as ticket sales or food concessions—from being used to secure more than 10 percent of the cost of the stadium.

The thinking was that the provision would force cities and states to find other sources of public revenue, like higher property taxes, hotel taxes or sales taxes, to finance stadiums, and that proposed increases in those taxes would get nowhere because politicians would be unwilling to anger citizens. But the law did not take into account the fan loyalty and pride that made new taxes politically acceptable, according to Dennis Zimmerman, a former Congressional Budget Office and Congressional Research Service analyst who is an expert on stadium financing.

"Congress thought putting this 10 percent rule in would kill it," Zimmerman said. "Nobody would expect taxpayers to hand over huge subsidies to these sports centers. But they did."

Since 2000, more than 45 sports stadiums were either built or renovated, according to a 2010 NCSL study. The average cost to build or renovate a stadium during this time was $412 million. Since the early 1960s, 91 sports stadiums have been built with public funding, and 22 of them were fully paid for with public funds. Twenty-nine of the publicly financed stadiums were funded through a hotel tax, 27 were funded through general obligations, 24 were funded through sales taxes, 23 were funded through bonds and four were funded from lottery or gambling revenues, NCSL said.

In a paper published in February, Moody's said both the growing popularity of professional soccer and the return of the NFL to Los Angeles County are "important drivers" of the increase in professional stadiums. After a lull in building from 2011 to 2015, stadium construction is on the upswing. Twice as many new stadiums, 12, are forecast to be completed over the next three years as were completed over the last five years, six, the report said. And most have at least some element of public financing.

New York Benefits

The value of bonds used to finance stadiums is influenced in part by how the team performs on the field. Better teams attract more fans, whose money is used to service the tax-free bonds.

One example is New York's $850 million Citi Field, opened in 2009 with the help of $616 million in public subsidies, including New York state municipal bonds. The "Let's go Mets!" cheers are louder at Citi Field lately, because fans are flocking to see a team that made a surprise run to the World Series last year.

The revenue from the healthy and growing number of fans led Moody's Investors Service to upgrade the stadium's bonds from a rating of Ba1, speculative and near "junk" status, to Baa3, a slightly higher rating that means the bonds are "investment grade." They are therefore more attractive to investors in the resale market. If the state were to refinance the bonds, it would pay lower interest and the better investment grade would lure more buyers.

With the upgrade, the bonds crossed the bond market equivalent of baseball's Mendoza Line, a derogatory term used for incompetent batters, usually those batting under .200.

Investors are more willing to buy highly rated bonds, just as baseball fans are more willing to support teams with better hitters.

"Ticket sales show performance today and performance in the future. If you make it to the World Series, every team but one in the last 14 years has experienced an increase in attendance of an average 10 percent," said John Medina, vice president and senior analyst for Moody's. (The exception was the San Francisco Giants in 2013, whose attendance dropped after winning the World Series in 2012.)

Across town, the new $2.3 billion Yankee Stadium, opened in 2009 with $1.2 billion in public money, also is considered a good investment (rated Baa2 by Moody's). Because while the team has not played particularly well in the past few years, it is so solid and established that its fan base and ticket sales are reliable as a revenue source.

In most cases, fans' spending on food, parking and luxury seat leases are included in bond rating criteria, but actual ticket sales are not.

But two IRS rulings specifically for the Yankees and the Mets made it possible for them to use ticket sales to secure bonds. (The Barclays Center in nearby Brooklyn, for example, home of the NBA Nets and NHL Islanders, can only use concessions, naming rights and premium seating to back up its bonds.) In addition, some stadiums have taxes on the tickets that are almost always used to finance public bonds for stadiums.

Richard Brodsky, a former New York state legislator who is now a senior fellow at New York University, said the fact that the Mets have a better team this year "is interesting in an academic way but it doesn't get to the complaint that this is corporate welfare. The average citizen gets screwed."

He bemoaned rising ticket prices, for example. MLB's average ticket price rose 7.1 percent in 2016, according to a survey by Team Marketing Report, a sports sales and marketing company.

"Bond holders are happy, that's fine; the people who are paying off the bonds are paying double what they used to pay for the same seats," he said.

> *"Politicians generally rationalize this*
> *expense by stating that stadiums*
> *will generate economic revenue*
> *and job opportunities for the city,*
> *but Kotkin says those promises are*
> *rarely realized."*

Cities Are Making Bad Investments on Sports Teams

Alexis Garcia

In the following viewpoint, Alexis Garcia argues that claims that new sports facilities bring revenue and employment opportunities to cities are false. The author uses interviews with several financial experts to make the claim that using municipal tax money to build owners new stadiums or to improve existing sports facilities creates only short-term, low-paying construction jobs and does not result in long-term economic benefits. Furthermore, the author asserts that the money could be used instead to improve roads or infrastructure and create permanent jobs to help the people of the community. Garcia is a producer at Reason TV.

"Sports Stadiums Are Bad Public Investments. So Why Are Cities Still Paying for Them?" by Alexis Garcia, Reason.com, March 17, 2015. Reprinted by permission.

As you read, consider the following questions:

1. How many regular-season NFL games can fans watch annually in new stadiums sometimes built using their tax dollars?
2. How much money did Wisconsin governor Scott Walker ask for to keep the Milwaukee Bucks from moving?
3. Does the author's use of interviews of public officials strengthen the viewpoint?

A nybody that drives around Southern California can tell you the infrastructure is falling apart," says Joel Kotkin, a fellow of urban studies at Chapman University and author of the book *The New Class Conflict*. "And then we're going to give money so a bunch of corporate executives can watch a football game eight times a year? It's absurd."

When the Inglewood City Council voted unanimously to approve a $1.8 billion stadium plan on February 24th, hundreds of football fans in attendance cheered for the prospect of a team finally returning to the Los Angeles area.

On its face, the deal for the city of Inglewood is unprecedented— Rams owner Stan Kroenke has agreed to finance construction of the stadium entirely with private funds. The deal makes the stadium one of the most expensive facilities ever built and is an oddity in the sports world, where most stadiums require millions in public dollars to be constructed.

And while the city still waits to hear if it will indeed inherit an NFL team, the progress on the new privately-funded Inglewood stadium has set off a bidding war between other cities that are offering up millions in public subsidies to keep (or attract) pro-sports franchises to their area.

St. Louis has proposed a billion-dollar waterfront stadium financed with $400 million in tax money to keep the Rams in Missouri. And the San Diego Chargers and Oakland Raiders have unveiled a plan to turn a former landfill in Carson, California, into a $1.7 billion stadium to keep the Rams from encroaching on their turf. While full details of the plan have yet to be released, it's been reported that the financing would be similar to the San Francisco 49er's deal in Santa Clara, which saw the team receive $621 million in construction loans paid for with public money.

Even the fiscally conservative Scott Walker is not immune to the stadium spending craze. The Wisconsin governor wants to allocate $220 million in public bonds to keep the Milwaukee Bucks basketball franchise in the area. Walker has dubbed the financing scheme as the "Pay Their Way" plan, but professional sports teams rarely pay their fair share when it comes to stadiums and instead use public money to generate private revenue.

Pacific Standard magazine has reported that in the last 20 years, the US has opened 101 new sports facilities and stadium finance experts say that almost all of them have received public funding totaling billions of dollars. Politicians generally rationalize this expense by stating that stadiums will generate economic revenue and job opportunities for the city, but Kotkin says those promises are rarely realized.

"I think this is sort of a fanciful approach towards economic development instead of building really good jobs. And except for the construction, the jobs created by stadia are generally low wage occasional work."

"The important thing that we've forgotten is 'What is the purpose of a government?'" asks Kotkin. "Cities instead of fixing their schools, fixing their roads or fixing their sewers or fixing their water are putting money into ephemera like stadia. And in the end, what's more important?"

Periodical and Internet Sources Bibliography

The following articles have been selected to supplement the diverse views presented in this chapter.

John Breech, "Rams Player Says NFL Should Look at Expanding Rather than Relocating Teams," CBS Sports, January 20, 2017. https://www.cbssports.com/nfl/news/rams-player-says-nfl -should-look-at-expanding-instead-of-relocating-teams/.

Richard Florida, "The Never-Ending Stadium Boondoggle," *CityLab*, September 10, 2015. https://www.citylab.com/equity/2015/09 /the-never-ending-stadium-boondoggle/403666/.

David Haugh, "2nd Team in Chicago? After Rams Move, What Is Shahid Khan Thinking?," *Chicago Tribune*, January 16, 2016. http://www.chicagotribune.com/sports/columnists/ct-rams-nfl -chicago-move-haugh-spt-0117-20160116-column.html.

Chris Rabb, "Professional Sports Teams Need a Better Ownership Model," Talking Points Memo, September 12, 2014. https:// talkingpointsmemo.com/cafe/professional-sports-teams-need -a-better-ownership-model.

Michael B. Sauter and Sam Stebbins, "Sports Teams Running Out of Fans," *USA Today*, January 30, 2016. https://www.usatoday.com /story/money/business/2016/01/30/sports-teams-running-out -fans/79466926/.

Rodger Sherman, "The Chargers Are a Case Study in Whether an NFL Team Can Survive Without Fans," Ringer, October 4, 2017. https://www.theringer.com/nfl/2017/10/4/16423520/los-angeles -chargers-owners-post-fan-experiment.

For Further Discussion

Chapter 1

1. Should parents direct their kids away from athletes as role models? If so, why? If not, why not? What other types of people might be better suited to be role models for kids?
2. Are athletes role models whether they like it or not, and must they behave accordingly? Or are they free to behave however they want, despite the influential positions they find themselves in?
3. What is the importance of role models for children? Must children have role models, or should they learn to behave well without them? Who have your role models been so far? Why did you look up to them? Did they serve their purpose?

Chapter 2

1. Should college athletes be paid for their services, given the revenue they generate for their universities and athletic programs, or is the scholarship money and often free education they receive a fair exchange for their athletic contributions?
2. Are professional athletes morally deserving of multi-million-dollar contracts? Make a case for why they deserve to be paid more than teachers or firefighters. Can you envision a society in which teachers make more money than professional athletes? How would that work?
3. Is the NFL right to ban guaranteed contracts, unlike the NBA and MLB? Explain your case, using examples from the viewpoints in this resource to support your argument.

Chapter 3

1. Should performance-enhancing drugs be legalized in professional sports? Would such a decision level the playing field or introduce a host of problems? Explain your stance with examples from this resource.
2. What arguments can be made for and against a salary cap in Major League Baseball? Pick a side and support it with research and examples from the viewpoints you've read. Then pick the opposite side and try to make an equally strong case.
3. Is competitive parity important, or is it more intriguing to have dominant teams? Explain your reasoning. If you were in charge of a sports league, what rules would you enforce regarding salaries?

Chapter 4

1. Do owners have the right to move their teams wherever and whenever they want? Should the players and fans get a say? Or should the market be the final determinant?
2. What would the benefits be of cities owning their own sports franchises? How would this work?
3. Should owners expect fans to pay for new stadiums in order to keep their teams? Why or why not? Is it fair for taxpayers to fund something that will ultimately make someone else richer? What other value can you see in taxpayer-funded stadiums?

Organizations to Contact

The editors have compiled the following list of organizations concerned with the issues debated in this book. The descriptions are derived from materials provided by the organizations. All have publications or information available for interested readers. The list was compiled on the date of publication of the present volume; the information provided here may change. Be aware that many organizations take several weeks or longer to respond to inquiries, so allow as much time as possible.

Major League Baseball (MLB)

245 Park Avenue, 31st Floor
New York, NY 10167
(212) 931-7800
website: https://www.mlb.com

The MLB is the governing body of its sport and has traditionally represented ownership. It represents all thirty teams, which are divided into three divisions in the American League and three more in the National League. The MLB deals with a myriad of issues, including player-owner relations, struggling franchises, sagging attendance, and potential rule changes.

Major League Baseball Players Association (MLBPA)

12 E. Forty-Ninth Street, 24th Floor
New York, NY 10017
(212) 826-0808
website: http://www.mlbplayers.com/

The MLBPA deals with all issues regarding major league baseball players, including contracts with owners, salary cap discussions, drug testing, sports betting, on-field safety, and a myriad of business affairs. The MLBPA is considered the strongest of all professional sports athlete organizations.

National Basketball Association (NBA)

645 Fifth Avenue, 19th Floor
New York, NY 10022-5928
(212) 407-8000
website: http://www.nba.com

The NBA is a league with thirty teams divided into six five-team divisions and two fifteen-team conferences. The league has grown in popularity in recent years through the star power of standouts such as Larry Bird, Magic Johnson, Michael Jordan, LeBron James, and Kevin Durant. It is dealing with several issues revolving around the salary cap and a lack of competitive parity.

National Collegiate Athletic Association (NCAA)

700 W. Washington Street
PO Box 6222
Indianapolis, IN 46206-6222
(317) 917-6222
website: http://www.ncaa.org

The governing body of major college athletics lists academics and athlete well-being as two of its priorities. The NCAA covers more than one thousand universities and one hundred conferences in Divisions I, II, and III. It creates rules and regulations followed by thousands of teams in dozens of sports.

National Football League (NFL)

345 Park Avenue
New York, NY 10154
(877) 635-7467
website: https://www.nfl.com

The NFL has been the most popular sports league in the United States for many years. The league is divided into the American Football Conference (AFC) and National Football Conference (NFC), both of which have sixteen teams. The league is dealing with several major issues, including franchise relocation and concussions that have resulted in long-term health issues for players.

NBA Players Association (NBPA)

1133 Avenue of Americas
New York, NY 10036
(212) 655-0880
website: https://www.nbpa.com

The NBPA represents all players competing in the National Basketball Association. It focuses on concerns of players such as contracts and the salary cap in place in the league, as well as available agents, codes of conduct, and the collective bargaining agreement currently in place.

NFL Players Association (NFLPA)

1133 Twentieth Street NW, #500
Washington, DC 20036
(202) 572-7500
website: https://www.nflpa.com

This union of National Football League players covers a wide variety of concerns, including ongoing concussion issues, the collective bargaining agreement with the league, player marketing and licensing, agent representation, and on-field rule changes.

Professional Golfers Association (PGA)

100 Avenue of the Champions
Palm Beach Gardens, FL 33418
(561) 624-8400
website: https://www.pga.com

The PGA is the all-encompassing body that oversees professional golf and golfers in the United States and beyond. All professionals are PGA members. The organization is responsible for player contracts and organizing tournaments while also providing services to amateurs such as technique tips and lessons.

US Olympic Committee (USOC)

1 Olympic Plaza
Colorado Springs, CO 80909
(719) 632-5551
website: https://www.teamusa.org

The USOC is the governing body of US Olympic teams and is overseen by the International Olympic Committee. The USOC supports and oversees American teams in not only the Winter and Summer Games, but also the Paralympics, Youth Olympic Games, and Pan American Games.

US Tennis Association (USTA)

70 W. Red Oak Lane
White Plains, NY 10604
(914) 696-7000
website: https://www.usta.com

The USTA is the governing body of professional and organized amateur tennis in the United States. It creates player rankings at both levels, runs tournaments, sets up leagues, provides information about lessons and coaching, and gives information about upcoming events.

World Anti-Doping Agency (WADA)

Stock Exchange Tower
800 Place Victoria, Suite 1700
Montreal, QC, Canada H4Z 1B7
(514) 904-9232
website: http://www.wada-ama.org

The World Anti-Doping Agency was founded with the aim of bringing consistency to anti-doping policies and regulations within sport organizations and governments throughout the world. Doping has been a concern for years in many national and international sports and sporting events, including the Olympics.

Bibliography of Books

James T. Bennett, *They Play, You Pay: Why Taxpayers Build Ballparks, Stadiums and Arenas for Billionaire Owners and Millionaire Players.* New York, NY: Springer Publishing, 2012.

Arthur Leonard Caplan and Bernard Parent, *The Ethics of Sport: Essential Readings.* New York, NY: Oxford University Press, 2017.

Eddie Comeaux, *College Athletes' Rights and Well-Being: Critical Perspectives on Policy and Practice.* Baltimore, MD: Johns Hopkins University Press, 2017.

Neil deMause and Joanne Cagan, *Field of Schemes: How the Great Stadium Swindle Turns Public Money into Private Profit.* Winnipeg, MB, Canada: Bison Books, 2008.

Rick Eckstein, *How College Athletics Are Hurting Girls' Sports: The Pay-to-Play Pipeline.* Lanham, MD: Rowman and Littlefield, 2017.

Charles C. Euchner, *Playing the Field: Why Sports Teams Move and Cities Fight to Keep Them.* Baltimore, MD: Johns Hopkins University Press, 1994.

Mark Fainaru-Wada and Lance Williams, *Game of Shadows: BALCO, and the Steroids Scandal That Rocked Professional Sports.* New York, NY: Avery, 2007.

Matthew Futterman, *Players: How Sports Became a Business.* New York, NY: Simon and Schuster, 2017.

Gilbert M. Gaul, *Billion-Dollar Ball: A Journey Through the Big-Money Culture of College Football.* New York, NY: Viking Press, 2015.

Gerald Gurney, Donna A. Lopiano, and Andrew Zimbalist, *Unwinding Madness: What Went Wrong with College Sports and How to Fix It.* Washington, DC: Brookings Institute Press, 2017.

Christopher S. Kudlac, *Fair or Foul: Sports and Criminal Behavior in the United States.* Santa Barbara, CA: Praeger, 2010.

Laurie Latrice Martin, *Pay to Play: Race and the Perils of the College Sports Industrial Complex.* Santa Barbara, CA: ABC-CLIO, 2017.

Mike McNamee, *Sport, Medicine, Ethics.* London, UK: Routledge, 2014.

David E. Newton, *Steroids and Doping in Sports: A Reference Handbook.* Santa Barbara, CA: ABC-CLIO, 2013.

Joe Nocera and Ben Strauss, *Indentured: The Inside Story of the Rebellion Against the NCAA.* New York, NY: Portfolio, 2016.

Dave Zirin, *Bad Sports: How Owners Are Ruining the Games We Love.* New York, NY: New Press, 2012.

Dave Zirin, *Game Over: How Politics Has Turned the Sports World Upside Down.* New York, NY: New Press, 2013.

Index

consumer sovereignty, described, 78–79

Covey, Stephen R., 34

D

Danielson, Michael N., 159

D.C. United, 169–170

defamation, defined, 92

Delany, Jim, 69–70

deMause, Neil, 168, 169–173

Dennis, Michael, 64–65

de Souza, Raymond J., 147, 148–150

diamond-water paradox, 85–86

diminishing utility, described, 86–88

Djokovic, Novak, 138

E

Elerson, Joe, 44, 45–48

Emmert, Mark, 70

English Premier League (EPL), 117–118

Epstein, David, 131, 132–136

ESPN, 164–165

ethical altruism, described, 96

ethical egoism, described, 95

F

Fischer, Jake, 70

Fisher, Derek, 126, 130

Frankowicz, Jakub, 151, 152–155

G

Gallan, Daniel, 36, 37–43

Garber, Don, 149

Garcia, Alexis, 181, 182–183

Garnham, Chase, 70

Gilbert, Dan, 93

Gladwell, Malcolm, 122–123

Goodell, Roger, 46, 47–48

Green Bay Packers, 158, 159, 160

H

Hatch, Nathan, 65

Hollis, Mark, 65

Houli, Bachar, 29

Howard, Sherman, 80

Hruby, Patrick, 158

I

Ingram, Murray, 42

J

James, LeBron, 90, 91, 92–93, 94, 95, 119, 121–122

K

Kaepernick, Colin, 41, 45, 47, 50–51, 52, 53

Katz, Daryl, 149

Kotkin, Joel, 182, 183

L

leadership

how coaches/parents can help student, 23–24

and responsibility, 23

Lewis, Lennox, 33

Lines, Gill, 39, 40

Los Angeles Rams, 157, 159, 175

Lynott, Beau, 161, 162–167

M

Major League Baseball (MLB)

collective bargaining agreement of, 105

doping in, and salary caps, 99–100

economic inequity in, 16–17, 102–108

increase in cost, to see games, 110

increase in salary/payroll of players/teams, after 1994 strike, 110–111

loss in diversity in, 111

luxury tax system of, 105–106, 107–108

Major League Soccer (MLS), 152–155, 169–170

Malone, Karl, 22

Mapfre Stadium (Columbus, OH), 153

market economy, described, 77–78

Matildas (Australian soccer team), 138

Mayweather, Floyd, 42

McCoy, Lesean, 48

McInerney, Mike, 38–39, 41, 43

Medina, John, 179

Miami Marlins, 102, 103

Miloch, Kimberly S., 71, 72–75

Mindock, Clark, 49, 50–53

Mitchell, Caesar, 176

Moody's Investment Service, 176, 178–179

Moore, Louis, 61

N

Nader, Ralph, 157–158

Napier, Shabazz, 59–60

National Basketball Association (NBA), 94

lack of competitive balance in, 126–127, 129–130

National Collegiate Athletic Association (NCAA), 63, 64, 65, 72, 73, 74

National Football League (NFL), 15–16, 45–48, 50, 53

Netto, Kevin, 137, 138–142

New York Mets, 104

New Zealand All Blacks, 37–38

Noll, Roger, 65, 172

Northwestern Business Review, 101, 102–108

O

objectification, described, 95

Odom, Lamar, 28

P

Pacific Standard, 183

Packer, Claire, 141

Pagels, Jim, 113, 114–124

Pastides, Harris, 69

performance-enhancing drugs
(PEDs)

in baseball, and salary caps,
99–100

in Olympic sports, 135

testing for, 132–136

in track and field, 134–135

Pilson, Neal, 64

Plonsky, Christine, 66–67

police brutality, 51

Political Research Quarterly, 60

Povich, Elain S., 174, 175–180

Precourt, Anthony, 152

R

Rapoport, Ian, 47

Reed, Ken, 156, 157–160

Robinson, Darius, 70

Rodriguez, Alex, 77, 134

salary in 2011, 104

Rogers, Robbie, 154

role models

definition of, 32

qualities of good, 33–34

shift in, in United States, 33

Rooney, Art II, 164

Rovell, Darren, 104–105

S

salaries

colleges should pay students,
58–60

debate over, student, 56

equity, and gender, 138–142

fans are reason for high athlete,
77–82

high, of athletes, 80–81, 84–89

percentage of total payroll, of
athletes across sports, 120–121

relationship between win rate
and, 104–105, 128–129

survey of public support for
student, 60

salary caps, in professional sports,
106–107

argument against, 119–120

argument for, 116–118

fairness of, debate over, 120–124

as form of collusion for team
owners, 114

game attendance and, 129

history of, 115–116

impact on competitive balance,
127–128

Schmidt, Martin, 127–128

Scott, Larry, 65

Shirley, Renee Ann, 133

Slive, Mike, 63–64, 69

Smith, Aaron, 37–38, 39

Smith, Adam, 85–86

Smoll, Frank L., 31, 32–35

Solomon, Jon, 62, 63–70

Southern Economic Journal, 121

sports franchise owners

have responsibility to
community, 148–150

and moving teams to other cities,
145–146, 152–155, 157–160,
162–167